COMPLETE CATALOGUE OF
AUSTIN CARS
since 1945

British Motor Industry Heritage Trust

COMPLETE CATALOGUE OF
AUSTIN CARS

since 1945

Anders Ditlev Clausager

Published 1992 by
Bay View Books Ltd
13a Bridgeland Street
Bideford, Devon EX39 2QE

© Copyright 1992 by Anders Ditlev
Clausager

Designed by Peter Laws
Layout by Gerrard Lindley
Typesetting by Chris Fayers

ISBN 1 870979 26 5
Printed in Hong Kong

Picture Acknowledgments

The great majority of the pictures
reproduced in this book are from the
archives of the British Motor Industry
Heritage Trust (Rover Group).
Pictures were also kindly supplied by
Nick Baldwin, Haymarket Publishing
and Jon Pressnell.

Contents

Left Austin's 1965 programme, the widest range offered by any British manufacturer – nine different saloon models spanning the price range from £500 to £3000, and that does not include sports cars and specialised vehicles.

Introduction

"You buy a car but you invest in an Austin", was the entirely appropriate slogan used by the Austin company for many years. To quote another period slogan, Austin cars were dependable. They were competently engineered, conservatively styled, and carefully made. They were frequently unexciting but they were rarely bad. Although the company was one of Britain's largest car-making concerns, Austin was not a national car in the same sense as for instance Fiat – it always had to share the top spot with arch rival Morris – but Austin nevertheless offered a wider range of models than any British competitor.

The company was founded by Herbert (later Lord) Austin, 1866-1941, in 1905. Formerly the general manager of the Wolseley company in Birmingham, Austin had designed a three-wheeled car in 1896, and the production Wolseleys made under the aegis of Vickers from 1901 were among the best-selling cars of their day. However, in 1905 Austin allegedly quarrelled with the Vickers management over the question of design, and left Wolseley to set up his own company at Longbridge on the southern outskirts of Birmingham. Among his backers were Frank Kayser, a Sheffield steelmaker, and the DuCros family of the Dunlop tyre company.

The first Austin car took to the road in 1906. From then until 1914, Austin made a series of predominantly large touring cars which did not greatly differ from other Edwardian cars. But Austins were well respected quality products, and the output from the Longbridge factory soon grew to rival older companies such as Daimler and Wolseley. In 1919 it was Herbert Austin's intention to concentrate on one new model, the Twenty, which had been designed for mass-production along the lines of American cars – although at the same time the company dabbled in commercial vehicles, tractors and even light aircraft. But the Twenty was too large and expensive for the British market, and brought the company close to bankruptcy.

The day was saved by the quick introduction of two other new models, the medium-sized Twelve and, in 1922, the Seven. The Seven was designed by Sir Herbert (he had been knighted in 1917) at his home, Lickey Grange, with the aid of a young draftsman, Stanley Edge (1903-1990). It was the first small British car to have a four-cylinder engine, of 747cc and rated at 8hp. It gave the Austin company a valuable lead over the competition and stayed in production until 1939, almost 300,000 Sevens being made.

Other new Austins were introduced during the 1920s and 1930s. The second most successful model was the Austin Ten, new in 1932, introduced at precisely the right time to cater for the changing tastes of British family car buyers. More than 180,000 Tens were made before the outbreak of war, the model outselling even the Seven at the height of its popularity. But there were bigger Austins as well, including a range of six-cylinder models topped by dignified limousines much beloved by the hire-car trade but also suitable as mayoral transport or for the staider type of dowager duchess. The company's best year before the war was 1937, with an impressive production of 89,000 cars.

The Seven had been almost revolutionary in 1922, and retained its slightly odd technical specification to the end, but otherwise pre-war Austins conformed to the undemanding standards prevalent in Britain in the 1930s. Other manufacturers might introduce independent front suspension, overhead-valve engines, hydraulic brakes or even unitary construction bodywork, but every Austin car before

Left The old man himself: Lord Austin in 1930, allegedly speaking on the telephone to the USA. His expression suggests that he is learning of further losses incurred by the American Austin company (which made Sevens under licence).

Below The most popular Austins, pre- and postwar, but even 300,000 Austin Sevens seem insignificant against the five million Minis.

Left Harry Austin, Lord Austin's brother, was a superintendent at Longbridge well into the 1950s. Here he shows off three generations of small Austins, the 1910 Seven single-cylinder, the 1923 Seven, and the New Seven of 1952.

1945 had beam axles and leaf springs, a side-valve engine, mechanical brakes and a separate chassis. By 1939 there were six models in the range, three fours and three sixes, spanning from 8 to 28hp, and usually available with a choice of body styles. Prices were competitive, ranging from £128 for the cheapest Austin Eight to £595 for the 28hp Ranelagh limousine. In terms of styling, Austin avoided the worst excesses of 1930s streamlining, and most models had a carefully nurtured family resemblance. The introduction in 1934 of a cowled radiator represented Austin's greatest leap forward of the decade.

However, even Austins were beginning to change. In 1938 Leonard Lord (later Lord Lambury, 1896-1967) had joined Austin as works director. For good or ill, Lord was one of the shapers of the British motor industry as we know it today. Of Yorkshire stock but born in Coventry, Lord was the most outstanding production man in the motor industry, and had earned his spurs with the Morris group of companies, becoming managing director and vice-chairman before quarrelling with Sir William Morris (Lord Nuffield) in 1936. Two years later, Lord's firm intention was to beat Morris at their own game, and from the

start he was clearly marked as Lord Austin's heir and successor. On Austin's death in 1941 Lord became joint managing director with E L Payton, and when Payton retired in 1945 he became sole managing director and chairman of the company.

Lord quickly mapped out his future plans for Austin but his intended programme of new models was only halfway completed before war broke out in 1939. He got Austin back into the commercial vehicle market with an all-new truck design in 1939 – it looked suspiciously like a contemporary Bedford but Lord was never a man to shy away from getting his inspiration elsewhere if it meant he could cut the development time of new products. The new Austin trucks had two significant features – an overhead-valve six-cylinder engine and hydraulic brakes. They were to prove tough and durable during the war years, when almost 100,000 Austin trucks were built, mainly for the armed forces.

Of Lord's planned new cars, a new Eight and a new Ten were introduced in early 1939. A new Twelve followed in August but hardly any were made before private car production was stopped by the war. In mechanical terms they were less of a departure from Austin traditions than the new

Below Leonard Percy Lord (Lord Lambury) was the guiding spirit behind Austin's successes after 1945.

Right In 1947 the new A40 range was still being assembled in the pre-war Trentham buildings. Dorsets on the left, Devons on the right, mostly with 'Export' stickers in the windscreens. The Sixteen assembly line is on the far right.

Above The Longbridge factory after the postwar extensions. On the extreme right are the old assembly halls (the Trentham buildings). In the centre are the postwar Car Assembly Buildings, the older CAB 1 behind, and CAB 2 in the foreground. On the left is the multi-storey car park.

Behind CAB 1 are, from left to right, the sales block (with the 'elephant house' behind), the admin block (the 'Kremlin'), and the engineering block.

trucks had been, but their styling was little short of radical by previous Austin standards, with rounded radiator grilles and alligator bonnets. All three models were re-introduced after the war, and Austin therefore had the advantage of having the newest (if not the most modern!) range of family cars in 1945. Furthermore, the Austin company stole a march on the competition by announcing its postwar model programme as early as November 1944. It was the first British manufacturer to do so, although prices for the postwar Eight and Ten were only announced in August 1945, and in October for the Twelve and the new Sixteen.

It is with this first postwar range that we start the detailed guide to post-1945 Austin cars.

Austin's postwar history may be neatly split up in four periods, each spanning approximately a decade. From 1945 to 1957 the company pursued its traditionally cautious product development and stayed rigidly within the prevailing conventions. It was rewarded by commercial success and the high noon of Austin came in 1952 when, under Leonard Lord's guidance, Austin emerged as the dominant partner in the merger with Morris which resulted in the formation of BMC. The number and variety of models produced

reflected Austin's position as general provider, with a home market share probably around 25%, but with great attention also being given to export markets.

The period from 1958 to 1968 saw Austin and BMC emerge as one of the technical leaders in the motor industry worldwide, with Alec Issigonis as chief designer and later technical director developing an outstanding range of front wheel drive cars, commencing with the Mini in 1959. Sadly, much of the original dynamism went out of BMC after Leonard Lord went into semi-retirement in 1961. His successor, George Harriman (1903-1973), must accept responsibility for BMC's muddle-headed product planning during the 1960s, which inevitably led to financial decline, and ultimately to

the unhappy merger with Leyland in 1968.

The Leyland years lasted from 1968 to almost 1980. For Austin, as for most of the other individual Leyland brand names, this was an unhappy decade. None of the major new models introduced was successful, and Austins began to lose their identity. The policies of the parent company were confusing or subject to rapid and bewildering changes. The oil crisis of 1973 was unhelpful, and Leyland's share of the home market was under ever-more effective attack from Ford, Vauxhall and the growing number of imports. With the effective nationalisation in 1975, Leyland (or BL) became a standing joke. But the nucleus of the original Austin empire, the vast factory at Longbridge, survived intact.

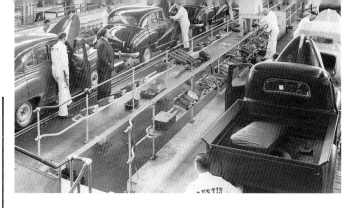

Above By 1952 CAB 1 was in full swing, accommodating assembly lines for the A30, A70 and A40 ranges. At the end of the lines hung an enormous painting of a dock scene, showing cars being loaded for export, with the exhortation "The ships are waiting".

Left Sir George Harriman took over from Len Lord in 1963. Remembered as a gentleman, during his reign Austin and BMC lost their momentum and finally fell into the grasp of Leyland in 1968.

Above By 1980 an Austin man was back in charge of Austin: the ex-apprentice Harold Musgrove, here waving off the BR loco 'Herbert Austin' in 1985, Austin's 80th anniversary year. Musgrove was replaced almost within a year of this.

Left Austin also made a wide range of commercial vehicles, up to 7 tons. This 1965 picture was taken in the then new commercial vehicle showroom, popularly known as the 'round-house' or the 'elephant house'.

An Austin renaissance dawned in 1977 when Michael Edwardes took over as chief executive of BL. One of Edwardes' ideas was to encourage the old marque names rather than subsume everything under a corporate Leyland identity. He found an able lieutenant and confirmed Austin man in Harold Musgrove, who was put in charge of BL's light-medium cars operation, which eventually became the Austin Rover Group. Edwardes and Musgrove were responsible for the new Austins of the 1980s, starting with the Mini-Metro, followed by the Maestro and Montego. Significantly better cars than their predecessors, this new Austin generation was an important first step towards bringing the ailing company round.

It was only a temporary reprieve. In 1986 Harold Musgrove and other senior executives were too openly opposed to a merger between the Austin Rover Group and Ford, and although they were able to frustrate this plan they paid with their jobs. A new chairman, Graham Day, arrived at BL, with a declared policy of moving the company up-market. By then only three of the many BL brand names remained – Austin, MG and Rover. It soon became clear that Rover, with its more up-market profile, was the preferred choice of name for the future. The company and all the new models would carry the Rover name. During 1987 the Austin badge was discreetly removed from current production. The original Metro was superseded by the new Rover version in 1990, and with the introduction of the Rover 200/400 series it became clear that the Maestro/Montego range only had a limited life ahead.

For another generation the Longbridge factory may still be 'the Austin' to local people, but it is now the Rover logo which greets you at the gate. Yet Longbridge is the tangible evidence of the Austin tradition and of the company's successes in the past. Not many of the pre-war buildings survive in unchanged form, but the result of Leonard Lord's great postwar expansion programme is clear for all to see – the administration block always known as the 'Kremlin', the round 'Elephant House' which was originally a commercial vehicle showroom, the engineering block, and the great assembly halls, CAB1 and CAB2 (short for Car Assembly Building). There is the multi-storey car park built in the early 1960s, the engine factory next door at Cofton Hackett (originally a late-1930s aircraft shadow factory), and, across the Bristol Road and the railway, the body plant or West Works, much extended and equipped with robots for the start of Metro production in 1980. And there have been further additions and improvements since.

Longbridge is the Austin legacy to the Rover Group, central and crucial to the company's present production and future plans. It is ironic then that the last Austins – the Maestro and Montego, even if they have lost the badge – are built in the erstwhile Morris factory at Cowley. But while both Cowley and Longbridge may soon only produce cars with the Rover (and MG?) badges, the heritage and traditions of the two great British mass manufacturers, Austin and Morris, have made significant contributions to the Rover Group of today and of the future.

Smallest of the 1945 models was the Eight, originally introduced in 1939, and postwar only made in four-door saloon form.

Eight, Ten, Twelve and Sixteen 1945-1949

Reproduced from a 1939 brochure illustration, this side view of the then new Ten shows its similarity to the Eight, only the increase in size and the additional ribs to the wings indicating any difference.

Of the first four postwar Austins, three had been introduced in 1939, although only the Eight and Ten had made any impact, the Twelve having been announced only a fortnight before war broke out. They were all very similar in design, with side-valve four-cylinder engines, beam axles with semi-elliptic leaf springs front and rear, and Girling mechanical brakes. The Eight had an engine first introduced in 1937 for the Austin Big Seven, while the Ten and Twelve engines went back to 1932. Thermosyphon cooling was getting rather old-fashioned by 1945, but only the Eight had a six-volt electrical system – acceptable by class standards – the bigger cars having twelve-volt systems. All had four-speed gearboxes with synchromesh on second, third and top.

In 1939 the Eight had been offered as a two-door saloon, and there had been tourer versions of both the Eight and the Ten. The Eight tourer was made in considerable numbers for the War Department in the period 1939-1942. The postwar versions were however only offered with four-door saloon bodies, of all-steel construction and with rather upright six-light styling. The alligator bonnets were still a novelty in Britain, while the rounded, chrome-plated radiator grilles with horizontal bars, together with the general shape of the bodywork, gave the Austins more than a passing resemblance to a scaled-down 1938 Buick.

One interesting feature shared by the Eight and Ten was that the body floor was integral with the chassis, providing a semi-platform chassis, with the body being bolted to the chassis forming substantial box-section side members. The similarly styled Twelve had a conventional chassis. This was a particularly roomy and well-equipped car, a worthy successor to the 'Heavy Twelve' of the 1920s, but the last of its line. Common features of all the postwar Austins were Zenith carburettors and mechanical AC fuel pumps, both to be retained well into the BMC period. The engines had conservative power outputs, and the three smaller-engined Austins had modest but adequate performance.

The new Sixteen was a different proposition. It had the chassis and body of the Twelve but a new engine, a 2.2-litre overhead-valve four. This was a derivative of the 1939 six-cylinder 3.5-litre truck engine and was developed during the war when Austin was asked to design an engine for a British equivalent of the jeep. Its chain-driven side-mounted camshaft, pushrod activated valves and whole layout would be the inspiration for the entire next generation of Austin engines – in other words, BMC engines through to the 1980s. Although the Sixteen ended

Not available for civilian consumption was this War Department Utility version of the Austin Ten.

That 'T' on the windscreen may indicate that this is an Austin Twelve, but apart from the badge on the radiator grille there was no external difference between the Twelve and the Sixteen.

up some 4cwt heavier than the Twelve, it had a considerable performance advantage and was capable of an honest 75mph. It was even better equipped than its stablemate and could be had with a heater and a radio. It also often came equipped with a sliding roof, as did the other Austins and indeed most early postwar British cars. In an era when most cars were uniformly black, Austins were available in blue, or grey, and the Sixteen in other colours as well.

Apart from the saloons, both the Eight and the Ten were available with van bodywork, and there was a wooden-bodied four-door shooting brake version of the Sixteen. In 1946 Austin bought the London coach-building firm of Vanden Plas, and an early idea was for Vanden Plas to produce a sports tourer based on the Austin Ten, but this came to nothing.

In 1946 the British motor industry celebrated its Golden Jubilee, and conveniently in time for this event Austin decided that they had made one million vehicles (a milestone reached by Morris in 1939, and by Ford a few months after Austin). The millionth Austin was one of the new Sixteens, painted cream and signed by all Austin employees including Leonard Lord. (Still preserved by the Rover Group Heritage Trust, the car is a restoration headache as it cannot be repainted.)

Export sales were becoming increasingly important to the British motor industry, with three major market areas being identified: Empire markets such as Australia, New Zealand and South Africa; North America, including Canada and the USA; and the European continent. Already well known in many countries worldwide before the war, Austin would greatly intensify its export drive from 1945 onwards, and publicity chief

Alan Hess undertook a number of headline-grabbing stunts to make the Austin name known abroad. His first, rather modest effort came in the severe winter of 1947, when a team of Sixteens started from Oslo in Norway and proceeded on a tour of seven capitals in seven days, finishing at Geneva in Switzerland for the opening of the motor show. Sammy Davis was one of the drivers on this trip, the first of several well-known motoring personalities who were persuaded to take part in Hess's projects.

While the Eight, Ten and Twelve were discontinued in 1947 to make way for the new A40 model, the Sixteen soldiered on into 1949, being built for the home market even after its replacement, the A70, had appeared at the 1948 Earls Court Motor Show.

A further step up in size from the Ten, the Twelve introduced a few weeks before war broke out was a particularly roomy and comfortable car for its class.

Specifications

EIGHT 1945-47
Engine four cylinder sv, 900cc
Bore × stroke 56.8×88.9mm
Power 27bhp @ 4400rpm
Transmission four-speed manual
Chassis semi-integral platform
Wheelbase 88.5in (2248mm)
Length 149in (3785mm)
Width 56in (1422mm)
Height 63in (1600mm)
Weight 1708lbs (775kg)
Suspension semi-elliptic leaf front and rear
Brakes mechanical
Bodywork four-door saloon, van
Top speed 61mph (98km/h)
Price when introduced £326
Total production 56,103

TEN 1945-47
Engine four cylinder sv, 1125cc
Bore × stroke 63.5×88.9mm
Power 32bhp @ 4000rpm
Transmission four-speed manual
Chassis semi-integral platform
Wheelbase 93.75in (2381mm)
Length 158in (4013mm)
Width 58.5in (1486mm)
Height 64.5in (1638mm)
Weight 1904lbs (864kg)
Suspension semi-elliptic leaf front and rear
Brakes mechanical
Bodywork four-door saloon, van
Top speed 62mph (100km/h)
Price when introduced £397
Total production 55,521

TWELVE 1945-47
Engine four cylinder sv, 1535cc
Bore × stroke 69.4×101.6mm
Power 42bhp @ 4000rpm
Transmission four-speed manual
Chassis pressed steel box section
Wheelbase 104.6in (2656mm)
Length 171in (4343mm)
Width 68in (1727mm)
Height 64.5in (1638mm)
Weight 2464lbs (1119kg)
Suspension semi-elliptic leaf front and rear
Brakes mechanical
Bodywork four-door saloon
Top speed 65mph (104km/h)
Price when introduced £531
Total production 8698

SIXTEEN 1945-49
Engine four cylinder ohv, 2199cc
Bore × stroke 79.4×111.1mm
Power 58bhp @ 3700rpm (later 67bhp @ 3800rpm)
Transmission four-speed manual
Chassis pressed steel box section
Wheelbase 104.6in (2656mm)
Length 171in (4343mm)
Width 68in (1727mm)
Height 64.5in (1638mm)
Weight 2912lbs (1322kg)
Suspension semi-elliptic leaf front and rear
Brakes mechanical
Bodywork four-door saloon, estate car
Top speed 75mph (121km/h)
Price when introduced £569
Total production 35,434

Above The actual 'Millionth Austin', the cream-coloured Sixteen which was signed by all Austin employees. The signature 'L P Lord' may be found prominently on the bonnet!

The Geneva Motor Show of 1947 was the first postwar motor show of any importance, and Austin chose to unveil the Sheerline and Princess models to an international audience on this occasion.

A few Sheerlines did find their way to the USA, although right-hand drive and a British number-plate behind the Massachusetts plate seem strange. British open golfer Henry Cotton used this Sheerline for a 1948 American tour.

Above Imposing car in genteel setting. The Sheerline pays a call.

Below The extended Sheerline limousine followed saloon styling faithfully.

A110/125 Sheerline and A120/135 Princess 1947-1956

None of the pre-war big sixes in the Austin range survived the war, for Leonard Lord had already been planning an up-to-date replacement in 1939. With Austin's traditions in the big car class a new big car was certainly expected, but the new postwar models caused a considerable degree of surprise when they were introduced at the 1947 Geneva Motor Show. They broke with Austin traditions in being aimed at the owner-driver rather than the carriage trade, and they introduced several new features which brought Austin engineering more or less up-to-date.

It is said that Leonard Lord aimed to challenge the Bentley. He drove an example of that make himself, while fellow Austin director E L Payton had a Rolls-Royce. Many features of the new cars seemed to have been inspired by these exalted ideals, not least the flying A radiator mascot which Austin stylist Dick Burzi designed along the lines of Bentley's winged B, on direct instructions from Lord. Italian-born Burzi, who had been with Austin since the late 1920s, was only really allowed to give of his best after Lord took over, and he was one of the better stylists working in the British industry in the dark ages before 1960. The Sheerline was one of his most inspired creations, with its traditional radiator topped by the flying A and flanked by Lucas P100 headlamps, graceful semi-razoredged body, flowing wing lines and gently curving tail.

The backbone of the new models was an immensely strong cruciform-braced box-section chassis. Their heart was the 1939 3.5-litre truck engine, very soon increased in capacity to 4 litres – hence the change in desig-nation from A110/A120 to the definitive A125/135. The extra horsepower of the Princess model were gained with the aid of a triple-SU carburettor set-up in place of the Sheerline's single Stromberg. It must have gone against the grain for Austin to buy carburettors from the rival Nuffield Organisation in the days before the merger! Notable firsts for Austin were the coil and wishbone independent front suspension, the fully-hydraulic Lockheed brakes, and the steering-column gearchange (a less appealing feature). It took Austin a long time to learn that column changes do not work very well with four-speed 'boxes.

Right The unique gas turbine-engined Sheerline of 1955.

Below The Sheerline limousine driver sat behind this down-market facia, rather like that of a Somerset or Hereford.

Above A convoy of new Austins leaves the factory in 1948. LPL registration for Leonard P. Lord?

Right An early Vanden Plas styling sketch for the Princess.

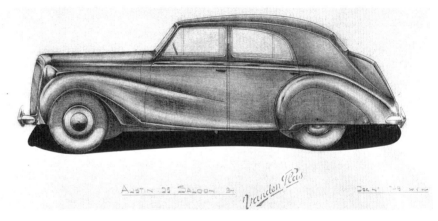

Apart from its more powerful engine, the Princess was distinguished by its coachbuilt body, made by Vanden Plas of Kingsbury in London. This firm had been bought by Austin in 1946, and for 40 years Vanden Plas would be synonymous with luxury Austins, even after the Kingsbury factory closed its doors in 1979. The cachet of coachbuilding to some extent explains the difference in price between Sheerline and Princess, but from a stylistic point of view the Princess was less successful. Its small built-in headlamps and less pronounced wing lines may have been more in keeping with 1947 fashion, but the end product was somehow not quite as satisfying as the Sheerline: high and wide, but not handsome. Vanden Plas also offered a touring limousine version of the Princess by the simple expedient of installing a glass partition between front and rear seats.

In 1949 a long-wheelbase Sheerline limousine followed, with elongated six-light coachwork built by Mann and Egerton at Norwich. Austin also made long-wheelbase chassis available to coach-builders specialising in hearses or ambulances, and some of these ended up with very peculiar bodywork. A standard Sheerline saloon was among the wedding presents of HRH

Princess Elizabeth and Prince Philip in 1947 (how odd it was not a Princess!), while the Queen of the Netherlands had a special touring car by a Dutch coachbuilder on a long-wheelbase Sheerline chassis. The Sheerlines did less well in the general export trade, with quite a number having to be shipped back from New York after failing to find American customers. By 1954 the Sheerlines were being phased out, though not before Austin had given some thought to a replacement with styling in the Somerset/Hereford mould. This remained abortive, as did a late facelift proposal which would have given the original Sheerline a longer nose and built-in headlamps.

The Princess in its original form lasted until 1956, with two interim facelifts: The Princess II of 1950 had a revised rear door with a reversed quarter-light, and the Princess III of 1953 had a new radiator grille. Later models had a single carburettor. The

touring limousine remained available until 1956. Production of the Princess was always on a modest scale, and more lasting success was achieved by the long-wheelbase limousine version introduced in 1952 (see description elsewhere in this book). The short-wheelbase saloon was replaced in 1956 by the Princess IV (also described elsewhere) which was an untypical Austin failure.

After its demise the Sheerline curiously made another niche for itself in Austin history as the basis for Austin's only attempt at building a gas turbine engined road car. This was demonstrated on the occasion of Austin's Golden Jubilee in 1955 but disappeared from sight almost immediately. The Sheerline was the only Austin car that could possibly have coped with the installation of the gas turbine engine, which was mainly conceived for stationary use and was indeed made and sold in some numbers.

Left "The rich arrived in pairs, and also in Rolls-Royces..." or in an Austin Princess. (Apologies to Hilaire Belloc!)

The Princess II had a very modest facelift, amounting to a new rear quarterlight.

By the time they brought out the Princess III, there were new front wings and an even more distinctive radiator grille – with, let it be said, a fibreglass surround.

Specifications

A110/125 SHEERLINE 1947-54
Engine six cylinder ohv, 3460cc (A110), 3993cc (A125)
Bore × stroke 85×101.6mm (A110), 87.3×111.1mm (A125)
Power 110bhp (A110), 125bhp (A125) @ 3700rpm
Transmission four-speed manual
Chassis pressed steel box section
Wheelbase 119.25in (3029mm)
Length 192in (4877mm)
Width 73in (1854mm)
Height 66in (1676mm)
Weight 4158lbs (1888kg)
Suspension independent coil front, semi-elliptic leaf rear
Brakes hydraulic
Bodywork four-door saloon
Top speed 82mph (132km/h)
Price when introduced £1279
Total production approx 8000

A125 SHEERLINE LIMOUSINE 1949-53
As A125 Sheerline except:
Wheelbase 132in (3353mm)
Length 204.2in (5186mm)
Height 67.5in (1715mm)
Weight 4536lbs (2059kg)
Bodywork limousine
Price when introduced £2140
Total production approx 700, plus 300 ambulance/hearse chassis

A120/135 PRINCESS 1947-50
As A110/125 Sheerline, except:
Power 120bhp (A120), 135bhp (A135) @ 3700rpm
Length 192.5in (4890mm)
Width 72.5in (1842mm)
Weight 4452lbs (2021kg)
Bodywork four-door saloon, touring limousine
Top speed 89mph (143km/h)
Price when introduced £1917
Total production 743 saloons, 57 touring limousines

A135 PRINCESS II 1950-53
As A135 Princess, except:
Weight 4342lbs (1971kg)
Top speed 86mph (138km/h)
Price when introduced saloon £1822, touring limousine £1981
Total production 669 saloons, 91 touring limousines

A135 PRINCESS III 1953-56
As A135 Princess II, except:
Price when introduced saloon £2292, touring limousine £2363
Total production 302 saloons, 48 touring limousines

The Princess facia resembled the Sheerline's, with an array of square dials, but the woodwork was different and two-tone upholstery was unique to the Vanden Plas-bodied car.

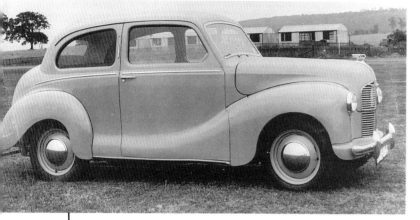

Above The sideview emphasizes the Burzi wing line. The dumpy six-light styling was not without similarities to the 1940 generation Chevrolet. This is the four-door Devon model.

Above Early version of the two-door A40 Dorset, always outsold by the Devon.

Right From the 1950 Montlhéry stunt when an A40 covered 10,000 miles in 10,000 minutes. The second-generation A40 had bigger headlamps with separate sidelamps.

A40 Devon, Dorset, Somerset, Sports and Commercials 1947-1956

When the British motor industry began to design new postwar cars it became the accepted wisdom that there would be a greater demand for bigger cars, particularly for export, and Austin and other manufacturers did not include 8hp cars in their immediate postwar plans, concentrating instead on larger models. It was therefore part of an overall trend when, in September 1947, Austin replaced the old Eight and Ten models (as well as the Twelve) with a single new design, the 1200cc A40. This move was also a response to the official exhortation for the industry to rationalise often complex and over-lapping model ranges – the government-proposed one company, one model policy.

The A40 was a cautious step forward. It still had a separate chassis but featured independent front suspension along the lines of the Sheerline and Princess models. On the other hand it used the Girling hydro-mechanical braking system. The new engine with overhead valves was a miniature version of the Sixteen unit but inherited the 3½in stroke

In common with many other new postwar cars, the original A40 used the very small Lucas 575 headlamps with built-in sidelamps. The radiator grille was derived from the 1939 pattern, still with a stylised winged wheel emblem, but this was now subservient to the flying A.

Above Under the A40 bonnet was this 1200cc overhead valve engine – an important piece of history, the ancestor of all BMC B-series engines.

Right A40 pick-up, in red/green/black Shell-Mex BP livery.

Above From May 1951, A40 commercials had a slightly different radiator grille with less chrome. This is a later example with the open rear wheel arch introduced in late 1952; the original models had spats over the rear wheels.

Left The revised Devon of 1951 was given a steering-column gearchange and this plain-Jane facia, which was very much a standard Austin design of the period.

Above The A40 Countryman – the first Austin estate car to use this famous name – was not terribly sophisticated, being simply a van with windows.

from the old Ten. It was the ancestor of the BMC B-series engine and that tell-tale stroke dimension would be found on all B-series engines to the end in 1980. A proposal to market a 3in narrower two-door version with a 1000cc engine as the A35 came to nothing; such a car could not really have been sold any cheaper.

The styling was more overtly American than the previous generation of Austins, being based on 1939-40 General Motors themes, still with a six-light configuration for the four-door Devon saloon. However, headlamps were built into the front wings, and Burzi's characteristic flowing wing line from the Sheerline was found also on the A40. The Dorset was a two-door version of the Devon, sold mainly for

export and discontinued in early 1949. Austin proudly announced: "Colour comes back to motoring", and the new cars were available in shades such as maroon, grey and light green.

Most of the early cars were exported. Austin found that the A40 was very acceptable to the North American public and shipped considerable numbers to Canada as well as to the USA. The A40 was advertised on the Gracie Fields show on American commercial radio stations. A privately-owned Dorset set up a new coast-to-coast record from Los Angeles to New York, and Goldie Gardner was one of a team of drivers who accomplished 10,000 miles in 10,000 minutes round a Long Island airfield, a stunt later repeated at Montlhéry in France. In Australia,

another important market, Devons were assembled from Completely Knocked Down kits and a unique locally-bodied A40 Tourer was available.

Commercial versions followed in 1948: a van, a pick-up, and an estate car – the first Austin 'Countryman' – which was simply a van with windows. These models retained the Devon-style front end and were to outlive the saloons by several years, being discontinued in 1956. The Devon underwent considerable change in 1951, receiving fully hydraulic brakes, a steering column gearchange in place of the floor-mounted lever, and a new dashboard with centrally-mounted instruments, but the model was beginning to look increasingly old-fashioned, and in early 1952, it gave

Left The 1952 Somerset was much more modern than the Devon but the rotund styling was still a little behind the times compared to other British cars of the period.

Above The Somerset interior was simple and unostentatious, with much painted metal in evidence.

The Somersets and Herefords kept the new assembly lines in Longbridge's Car Assembly Building busy. This was considered to be the most modern car factory in Europe at the time, and the gentleman on the left is obviously wielding a very high-tech piece of instrumentation; but note the low-tech hammer in his overall pocket!

way to the Somerset.

This had four-light styling and was rather rotund, in the same mould as the A70 Hereford and A30 Seven. The wider doors greatly improved access, particularly to the rear seat. The characteristic swept wingline was still featured, and the radiator grille was still a recognisable descendant of the 1939 style. The chassis and engine were little changed from late-model Devons. In addition to the saloon, Austin brought out a two-door drophead coupé with a body made by Carbodies in Coventry. Both models continued in production until 1954.

There had been an additional model in the A40 range from 1950 to 1953, the A40 Sports. For some years there had been close relations between Austin and the Jensen company at West Bromwich; Austin sold the big 4-litre engines and other mechanical components to Jensen for use in their luxury saloons. Jensen developed a

design for a large sports tourer and sports saloon which they put on the market as the first Interceptor, and a scaled-down version of this style was fitted to an Austin Devon chassis, becoming the A40 Sports. Apart from a tuned engine with two SU carburettors there was little change mechanically. The Sports followed the changes made to the Devon, receiving fully hydraulic brakes and a steering-column gearchange in 1951.

The Sports chassis were produced at Longbridge and were then sent across to Jensen to be fitted with bodywork. As with other models in the range, a considerable proportion was exported, but the Sports was always a limited production model, as there was no great demand for what was actually a rather unsporting four-seater tourer. An A40 Sports did however become involved in a typical Alan Hess stunt. He accepted a half-a-crown bet from Leonard Lord that he could not take an

Austin car around the world in a month. He did the job in three weeks in June 1951, by dint of employing a KLM Skymaster to fly the car across the oceans and other tricky bits. The car still covered 9,263 miles, an average of 441 miles for each of the 21 days, including the flying time.

Above The A40 Sports was a 'custom' Austin with a body from an outside coachbuilder, in this case Jensen of West Bromwich. The family relationship to the much larger Jensen Interceptor is evident.

Above With the hood down, the A40 Sports reveals the four-seater accommodation. Despite the 'sports' title it was more of a modern replacement for the pre-war Austin Ten tourer.

Carbodies in Coventry supplied the bodies for the drophead coupé versions of the Somerset and the very similar A70 Hereford.

Specifications

A40 DEVON/DORSET 1947-52
Engine four cylinder ohv, 1200cc
Bore × stroke 65.5×88.9mm
Power 40bhp @ 4300rpm
Transmission four-speed manual
Chassis pressed steel box section
Wheelbase 92.5in (2350mm)
Length 153.25in (3893mm)
Width 61in (1549mm)
Height 63.75in (1619mm)
Weight 2128lbs (966kg)
Suspension independent coil front, semi-elliptic leaf rear
Brakes hydraulic front, mechanical rear (all hydraulic from 1951)
Bodywork two-door saloon (Dorset), four-door saloon (Devon), estate car, van, pick-up
Top speed 71mph (114km/h)
Price when introduced £403 (Dorset), £416 (Devon)
Total production 273,958 Devons, 15,939 Dorsets, approx 26,587 Countrymans, approx 78,242 vans, approx 61,818 pick-ups

A40 SOMERSET 1952-54
As late-model Devon, except:
Power 42bhp @ 4500rpm
Length 159.5in (4051mm)
Width 63in (1600mm)
Height 64in (1626mm)
Weight 2142lbs (972kg)
Bodywork four-door saloon, drophead coupé
Top speed 68mph (109km/h)
Price when introduced £728 (saloon), £775 (drophead coupé)
Total production 166,063 saloons, 7243 drophead coupés

A40 SPORTS 1950-53
As Devon/Somerset, except:
Power 46bhp @ 5000rpm
Length 159.25in (4045mm)
Width 61.25in (1556mm)
Height 57.5in (1461mm)
Weight 2060lbs (935kg)
Bodywork open four-seater
Top speed 79mph (127km/h)
Price when introduced £818
Total production 4011

The A70 Hampshire was a bigger version of the Devon, but the rear wheel spats and, on this example, the two-tone colour scheme helped to set it apart.

Very much built with export markets such as Australia in mind, the A70 pick-up was quite a rugged sort of vehicle.

A70 Hampshire, Hereford, Countryman and Pick-up 1948-1954

A year on from the Devon, Austin rounded off their postwar range with the introduction of the A70 Hampshire saloon, one of two new models introduced in time for the first postwar Earls Court Motor Show in October 1948. The Hampshire offered few surprises for contemporary students of Austin development. It used the overhead-valve 2.2-litre engine from the Sixteen in a new chassis with a wheelbase only slightly longer than the A40, while the independent front suspension and hydro-mechanical brakes followed the smaller car's design.

Styling was also similar, with a six-light saloon body, but the line of the wing was higher up, the boot was more pronounced, there were spats over the rear wheels, and the car was noticeably broader in the beam – a proportion which was accentuated by the headlamps being set further into the front wings than on the Devon. Fitted from the start with a steering-column gearchange and a split-bench front seat, the Hampshire was intended as a full six-seater and was wide enough

for it, but the short wheelbase restricted body length and in consequence legroom. On the other hand, compact dimensions gave the car a respectable performance and the Hampshire had a top speed higher even than the Sheerline. Unfortunately, the handling was almost as lively as the performance.

This was one of those cars which the British industry developed after the war with an eye to export markets. The Standard Vanguard was the classic example of the breed, but the Humber Hawk was built to the same formula:

all of them were relatively compact cars but capable of seating six passengers, and with good performance from powerful four cylinder engines of around two litres. This type of car did very well for Britain in Empire markets such as Australia, but when General Motors developed Australia's own car, the Holden, and

The A70 Hampshire-style Countryman was at least partially a 'woody'. With its four doors it was a more practical and less van-like vehicle than the A40 Countryman.

The A70 Hereford of 1950 pioneered the next-generation Austin look, with its four-light styling and well-rounded lines, later reflected by the Somerset and A30 models.

The hood of the Hereford drophead coupé could be supplied with power operation, like that of the contemporary Ford Zephyr convertible, also bodied by Carbodies.

The Hereford had a more plush interior than for instance the Somerset and was almost a full six-seater.

the Australian government introduced severe tariffs to protect their home-based industry, the British contenders lost out. While the Holden was built to the same formula as the Hampshire or Vanguard, it had the added refinement of a six-cylinder engine. Among British postwar cars in the two-litre class, the Vauxhall Velox was first with a six-cylinder engine, soon followed by the unsuccessful Morris Six, and after Ford brought out the Zephyr Six in 1950 the rest of the industry had to fall into line sooner or later.

Austin was not to field a medium-sized six before late 1954, by which time the significance of the export trade, particularly to Australia, had diminished somewhat and the accent was once again on meeting new home market requirements in the upper echelons of the family car market. The four-cylinder A70 had therefore to serve a six-year term. The Hampshire lasted a mere two years, being replaced at the 1950 Motor Show by the Hereford. This pioneered the next generation of Austin styling with its curvaceous lines and four-light configuration, later also adopted for the A40 Somerset and in small-scale form for the A30 Seven. The chassis and engine were not greatly changed but the Hereford enjoyed the benefit

of fully hydraulic brakes, while another 3 inches in the wheelbase did something to improve the legroom. While the Hereford usually had a steering column change, a small number of cars were built to Police orders with a floor change, borrowing the gearbox from the Austin Taxi.

There were Countryman versions of both Hampshire and Hereford with semi-wooden bodywork, but both were rarities and the majority went for export. Also an unusual sight in its

native country was the pick-up version, again made with either Hampshire or Hereford styling – one imagines that this model was mainly intended for Australia where the 'ute' was and is part of everyday life in the bush. The only other alternative bodystyle was the Hereford drophead coupé, with a Carbodies body similar to the A40 Somerset drophead, and with the option of a power-operated hood as found on the original A90 Atlantic. This model had only a limited

This all-steel Countryman based on the Hereford is possibly a special body; normally the A70 Countryman had a semi-wooden body.

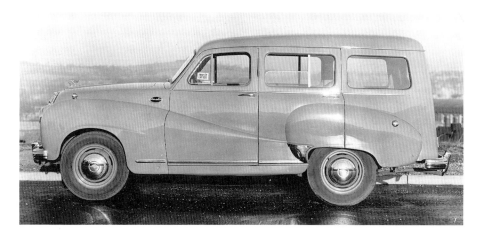

The Pick-up version combined style and good performance with a payload capacity of 15cwt in a load area over 5 feet long. It was always most popular in export markets, and could also be supplied in chassis/scuttle or chassis/cab form.

The standard A70 Countryman based on the Hereford style had this four-door body partly constructed in wood. Incidentally, the Countryman and Pick-up models were never referred to as Herefords or Hampshires, these names being exclusive to the saloon models.

production run, much shorter than the Somerset drophead's.

A Hampshire had its moment of glory, being used for another of the Austin record runs. Ralph Sleigh and Peter Jopling set up a new record for the England to Cape Town run of just over 24 days in November and December 1949, beating the 1939 record of Symons and Browning who had covered the 10,300 mile journey in 32 days in their Wolseley. Extra fuel tanks gave the Hampshire a capacity of 57 gallons, and the front seats could be converted to a bed; otherwise no major modifications were made.

The A70 series came to an end in 1954. With production figures so much lower than the A40 models, and probably a larger proportion of the cars being exported, the Hampshires and Herefords are now among the rarest Austins of the early postwar period.

Specifications

A70 HAMPSHIRE 1948-50
Engine four cylinder ohv, 2199cc
Bore × stroke 79.4×111.1mm
Power 67bhp @ 3800rpm
Transmission four-speed manual
Chassis pressed steel box section
Wheelbase 96in (2438mm)
Length 163.25in (4147mm)
Width 66.4in (1686mm)
Height 65in (1651mm)
Weight 2800lbs (1271kg)
Suspension independent coil front, semi-elliptic leaf rear
Brakes hydraulic front, mechanical rear
Bodywork four-door saloon, estate car, pick-up
Top speed 83mph (134km/h)
Price when introduced £608 (saloon)
Total production 34,360 saloons, 901 estate cars, approx 20,434 pick-ups (including Hereford-type pick-ups)

A70 HEREFORD 1950-54
As A70 Hampshire, except:
Wheelbase 99in (2515mm)
Length 167.5in (4255mm)
Width 69.6in (1768mm)
Height 65.6in (1667mm)
Weight 2827lbs (1283kg)
Brakes hydraulic
Bodywork four-door saloon, drophead coupé, estate car, pick-up
Top speed 80mph (129km/h)
Price when introduced £738 (saloon), £1122 (drophead coupé)
Total production 48,640 saloons, 1515 estate cars, 266 drophead coupés (pick-ups, see A70 Hampshire)

Dick Burzi (peeking over the model) and Leonard Lord (on the right) examine a clay scale model of their most daring effort, the A90 Atlantic.

The prototype Atlantic had this one-piece wind-screen, which had to be given up for production. It was not short of Austin insignia, including no less than four of the 'Austin of England' script badges.

A90 Atlantic 1948-1952

In strictly commercial terms, the Atlantic was a fiasco. Its styling was and is controversial. It was not a particularly good car, and its engine was subsequently put to much better use in the Austin-Healey 100. But no-one can deny the tremendous impact the car had, and it has earned a deserved following among enthusiasts. If nothing else, one must admire the sheer bravado of Leonard Lord and the Austin company for producing a car such as this.

It was always Austin's problem, compared to Nuffield, Rootes or Standard-Triumph, that it only had one brand name for its range. Where other British manufacturers could conveniently market their prestige models under one of their subsidiary labels secure in the knowledge that a Humber would command greater respect than a Hillman, or that an MG was automatically assumed to be more sporting than a Morris, Austin was stuck with just its own name, which had to cover everything from baby cars to limousines. Perhaps this is why the poor old Atlantic attracted so much more opprobrium than the Triumph Roadster or the Riley 2½-litre Roadster.

It was in fact far more successful than either. Not that that is saying much.

The reason for the Atlantic was Leonard Lord's obsession with the American market, understandable at a time when all British car manufacturers were hell-bent on selling their products for hard currency. Lord had a taste of sweet success with the A40, and this spurred him on to making even greater efforts to capture American customers. The MG sports car was just beginning to make its presence felt in the USA. Lord

reckoned that anything the competition could do, he could do better. So he told Dick Burzi that he wanted a sports version of the new A70, using the same chassis but with a flashier body job. Apparently Austin somehow got hold of a new Alfa Romeo with a Pinin Farina convertible body, and this became the inspiration for the Atlantic. It is difficult to imagine how they got the import permit but they probably bent several rules. Perhaps this was the reason why the Alfa was later disposed of on

This olde-English half-timbered pub is a slightly unlikely background for the futuristic Atlantic, but the Mitchells and Butlers Ales were (and are) as homely to Brummies as Austin cars. Note the modified windscreen on this production model, with separate curved end pieces.

Almost for the first time under an Austin bonnet, twin SU carburettors – rank heresy to the faithful at Longbridge. Note the massive radio amplifier next to the battery.

favourable terms to American stylist Holden Koto who was brought in to design the A30.

The Atlantic was Burzi at his most extravagant. The front end might have been inspired by the Tatra, with three headlamps above the narrowest of air intakes. The Atlantic had not one but two flying As perched precariously on the curving bonnet like skiers about to commence the downhill run. The Austin wing line was given full rein, the front wing sweep running all the way back to the rear bumper. No rear wings were permitted to mar the perfection of the line, and the rear wheels were scarcely visible, hiding behind shallow spats which made wheel changing particularly tiresome. A chromium waterfall adorned the bonnet – this was a straightforward crib from Pontiac – and while it had been the intention to give the car a compound-curve one-piece windscreen, for ease of production it became necessary to split it in three, with separate end pieces.

The Atlantic was originally conceived only as a convertible, but a commodious one, seating five (not quite six; the rear seat was too narrow). Options included power-operated hood and windows – notable firsts for a British mass-production car – and this clearly indicated that the car was

The facia lay-out resembled that of the Hampshire but the Atlantic had fancy gold-painted dials and featured a rev. counter. Smokers were well provided for.

Messrs Buckley, Goodacre and Hess pose with the Atlantic at the Indianapolis Speedway.

During the Indianapolis record run, the original bonnet was damaged when it blew open, so a bonnet in another colour from a spare car was substituted. To this day, the car carries this bonnet complete with commemorative plaque.

The Atlantic saloon was a bit of an afterthought. It featured a vinyl-covered roof, the rear window was also split in three and its centre section could be lowered.

primarily aimed at the USA, as did the name and the New York skyline backdrop used in the original brochure artwork. The instruments were gold-faced and included a rev. counter. To give the car a definite performance edge over the A70, the engine was bored out to 2.6 litres and fitted with two SU carburettors.

To give the model a flying start in the USA, an early Atlantic was taken out to the Indianapolis speedway in April 1949 with the aim of setting up a new series of official American stock car (production car) records. This was another Alan Hess inspiration, and he brought Sammy Davis out to oversee the pit work, while drivers were Dennis Buckley, Charles Goodacre and Hess himself. The first attempt had to be abandoned after 35 hours when someone forgot to put water in the radiator, but after a change of engine the team started again and completed 11,850 miles at an average of 70mph over seven days and nights. The Atlantic proved capable of 90mph and duly took 63 assorted records. Sadly, this impressive performance was to no avail, nor could a $1,000 price reduction improve the Atlantic's chances in the USA – Austin sold exactly 350 Atlantics there. The car could not compete with the local breed

of V8-engined luxury convertibles which cost no more.

Eventually, most Atlantic production was diverted to other export markets or to the home market. In late 1949, a sports saloon version was introduced, and in 1950 the model was given fully hydraulic brakes to keep up with A70 developments. The convertible was discontinued in 1951 and the saloon soldiered on to the end of 1952. The reason then given for the model's demise was that it had been decided to rationalise the model range after the Austin-Morris merger. This was somewhat of a white lie... There would never be another Austin quite as exuberant as the Atlantic again.

Specifications

A90 ATLANTIC 1948-52
Engine four cylinder ohv, 2660cc
Bore × stroke 87.3×111.1mm
Power 88bhp @ 4000rpm
Transmission four-speed manual
Chassis pressed steel box section
Wheelbase 96in (2438mm)
Length 177.1in (4499mm)
Width 70in (1778mm)
Height 60in (1524mm) convertible, 61in (1549mm) saloon
Weight 2828lbs (1284kg) convertible, 2996lbs (1360kg) saloon
Suspension independent coil front, semi-elliptic leaf rear
Brakes hydraulic front, mechanical rear (all hydraulic from 1950)
Bodywork convertible (1948-51), two-door sports saloon (1949-52)
Top speed 92mph (148km/h)
Price when introduced £953 (convertible), £1017 (saloon)
Total production 7981 (approximately half convertibles, half saloons)

The very simple interior of the FX3 offered somewhat cramped accommodation for the driver, while instruments were similar to the 1945 generation of Austin cars.

The post-war Austin Taxi bore some resemblance to the Austin Sixteen whose engine it used but the radiator was more like Austin's contemporary trucks. This is the classic London type with the open luggage platform.

A taxi that isn't; special-bodied FX3s such as this all-wood shooting brake would have found favour with Northern land-owners to whom a 'shooting brake' was still exactly that.

Taxi and Hire Car 1948-1981

It is no secret that relations between BMC people and Leyland people were a little strained after the merger of the two companies in 1968. Soon after, a meeting was held at Leyland's headquarters in London with both BMC and Leyland managers attending. As was then usual, the main point on the agenda was BMC's alleged deficiencies. Finally, an old-school BMC senior manager said to his new colleagues, "You can say what you like about us but you can't deny we always had a much bigger market share. Why, you only have to look out of the window and I'll bet you that nine out of ten cars you see are BMC products". With boos and cries, the Leyland people leapt as one to the window, and saw the square below teeming with black Austin taxis.

Austin began to take a serious interest in the London taxi market in 1930 when a special version of the 'Heavy Twelve' chassis was made available to a variety of coachbuilders. The regulations for London taxis are unique and impose severe restrictions on manufacturers wishing to enter this market, the most famous of which is the requirement for a 25ft turning circle. But the Austins were extremely successful and by 1939 had a dominant position in this specialised field, with sales far outstripping rivals such as Morris-Commercial or Beardmore.

Prototypes for a new design were being developed soon after the war but it was not until early 1949 that the first new Austin FX3 began to ply for fares. This model used the 2.2-litre engine from the Austin 16 and A70 models in a special chassis with leaf springs front and rear and the seemingly archaic feature of mechanical brakes. Austin now supplied the vehicle complete with bodywork made by the Coventry firm of Carbodies. In addition to the Taxi model, a 'provincial hire car' was offered, type designation FL1. This differed from the London taxi in having a nearside front door and a front passenger seat instead of the open luggage platform stipulated under the London regulations. Both vehicles had the traditionally roomy rear compart-ment, with a rear seat for two to three passengers and two folding occasional seats on the central division.

Although the FX3 was principally aimed at the London market and those English provincial cities which had similar taxi regulations, some attempts were made at exporting it and a few examples could even be found plying for hire in New York. They were however soon rejected by New York cabbies, who preferred the more softly sprung American Checkers. The Austins did not have much success in European cities apart from Madrid – but the London market was big enough to warrant making such a specialised type. The taxis were usually handled by the old-established firm of Mann and Overton in London, and by selected distributors in the larger provincial cities.

In the autumn of 1954 the new BMC 2.2-litre diesel engine was made available in both the taxi and hire car types, immediately becoming extremely popular, so that from then on sales of the diesel-engined taxi always greatly outstripped those of the petrol model. This undoubtedly contributed to Austin's decision to make their next generation taxi, the FX4 launched in 1958, available only with a diesel engine. The FX4 was also notable for having a fully automatic Borg Warner gearbox as standard, and other mechanical features included inde-pendent front suspension with coil springs and wishbones, as well as hydraulic brakes. FX4 styling was quite up-to-date by the standards of the late 1950s. The body was built out to the

The 1958 redesign brought the taxi into line with contemporary car styles. This 1966 example still features the original roof-mounted indicators, and a purdah glass rear window was a popular option.

The way we were... London street scene, circa 1972. Fashions have changed rather more than taxis.

full width of the vehicle, and a nearside front door was fitted. The expected hire car version, the FL2, followed in 1959.

A manual-gearbox alternative was offered from 1961 onwards, and in 1962 a petrol-engined version finally appeared, reinstating the old 2.2-litre engine which was by now only used in the Austin Gipsy and some BMC commercial vehicles such as the LD range. The petrol-engined taxi and hire car were made only with the manual gearbox. The taxi continued through the 1960s with very little in the way of alteration, although later models from 1970 onwards could be distinguished by the absence of roof-mounted indicators and by their modified tail light units, which were in fact shared with the 1100/1300 Mark II range. In 1971 the 2.2-litre diesel unit was replaced by a more powerful 2.5-litre engine, and two years later the petrol engine option was discontinued.

In its day the FX3 had also been available in chassis form, and some shooting brake type vehicles were made on this basis, as well as newspaper delivery vans. The FX4 was more rarely seen with alternative body styles, except for a few newspaper delivery vans, but notable was the very special town car which the eccentric millionaire Nubar

Gulbenkian had built on an FX4 chassis, in a style harking back to the days of horsedrawn carriages.

Austin continued to enjoy a virtual monopoly of the London cab business during the 1970s, competitors such as the postwar Nuffield Oxford, the Beardmore and the Winchester having virtually disappeared. Some consideration was given to developing a replacement but this never got further than some styling mock-ups in the early 1970s. Gradually the manufacture of the FX4 was more and more farmed out to Carbodies, who took over the chassis build as well as the body construction, British Leyland only supplying the engines and other mechanical components. Finally at the beginning of the 1980s an agreement was reached whereby the erstwhile Austin Taxi would become a Carbodies Taxi, and as such the FX4 continues to this day, now fitted with diesel engines supplied by Land Rover. It is the oldest Austin design in current production, beating the Mini by a few months, and despite recent competition from the Metrocab its hold on the London cab market is as strong as ever.

Specifications

FX3/FL1 series 1948-58
Engine four cylinder ohv, 2199cc
Bore × stroke 79.4×111.1mm
Power 52bhp @ 3800rpm (taxi), 68bhp @ 3800rpm (hire car)
Transmission four-speed manual
Chassis pressed steel box section
Wheelbase 113.6in (2886mm)
Length 173.25in (4401mm)
Width 67.5in (1715mm)
Height 70.75in (1797mm)
Weight 3192lbs (1449kg)
Suspension semi-elliptic leaf front and rear
Brakes mechanical
Bodywork five-seater taxicab, seven-seater hirecar
Top speed 60mph (96km/h)
Price when introduced £994 (taxi, complete), £972 (hire car)
Total production approx 13,500 (inc. Diesel-engined models)

FX3D/FL1D series 1954-58
As FX3/FL1 series, except:
Engine four cylinder ohv Diesel, 2178cc
Bore × stroke 82.6×101.6mm
Power 55bhp @ 3500rpm
Price when introduced £1013 (taxi)
Total production see petrol model

FX4D/FL2D series 1958-71
Engine four cylinder ohv Diesel, 2178cc
Bore × stroke 82.6×101.6mm
Power 55bhp @ 3500rpm
Transmission automatic (four-speed manual optional)
Chassis pressed steel box section
Wheelbase 110.6in (2810mm)
Length 179.75in (4566mm)
Width 68.6in (1743mm)
Height 69.5in (1765mm)
Weight 3528lbs (1602kg)
Suspension independent coil front, semi-elliptic leaf rear
Brakes hydraulic
Bodywork five-seater taxicab, seven-seater hirecar
Top speed 75mph (121km/h)
Price when introduced £1876
Total production (to end of 1981) approx 43,000 of all models

FX4/FL2 series 1962-73
As FX4D/FL2D series, except:
Engine four cylinder ohv, 2199cc
Bore × stroke 79.4×111.1mm
Power 56bhp @ 3750rpm
Transmission four-speed manual only
Price when introduced £1514
Total production see FX4D/FL2D above

FX4D/FL2D series from 1971
As 1958-71 model, except:
Engine four cylinder ohv Diesel, 2520cc
Bore × stroke 88.9×101.6mm
Power 60bhp @ 3500rpm
Transmission automatic only
Length 180.5in (4585mm)
Total production see FX4D/FL2D above

Below This is a production model of the first A30 (AS3 series) as it made its bow at the Motor Show in October 1951. A little less rotund than the contemporary Somersets and Herefords but clearly a member of the Austin family.

Above A very early A30, with the numberplate showing the original model designation. This car must be a prototype as it appears to have the fuel filler cap on the nearside, not visible here. Note also the single wiper.

A30 and A35 1951-1968

Austin's immediate postwar plans did not call for a really small car, and for four years the A40 Devon was the smallest model in the range. However, when it became clear that Morris had a winner on their hands in the shape of the new Morris Minor, it became inevitable that Austin would rejoin the battle. In 1948 Leonard Lord paid the handsome sum of £10,000 to Ian Duncan for the Dragonfly prototype – an advanced two-seater small car which featured unitary body construction, a transverse engine, front wheel drive and rubber suspension. This was deemed a little too advanced for the immediate future, and the Longbridge designers turned to a more conventional small car, although the decision was made to give the new model a unitary body – Austin's first.

The layout of the car was based, perhaps too closely, on the late 1930s Austin Seven Ruby saloon. A new 800cc engine, following the design of the A40 unit, was developed for the new model and was later to become famous as the BMC A-series. Suspension and steering followed established Austin practice. A cost-saving expedient was to use but a

Right In late 1953 the A30 range was supplemented by this two-door version and several other changes were introduced at the same time, heralding the AS4 series (or in two door form, A2S4 series). Two-tone colour schemes were not quite standard, however.

single hydraulic cylinder for both rear wheel brakes, mounted under the rear seat pan with a mechanical linkage to the brake drums. Other cost-saving features were the external door hinges, windows which slid rather than wound down, and on early cars a single rear lamp and a no-key ignition switch.

For the styling of the new small car Austin – unusually at that time – employed an outside consultant. This was Raymond Loewy Associates, the American group best known in Britain for their work for the Rootes Group. Loewy sent stylist Holden Koto to Longbridge in 1950. The Loewy-Koto proposal was initially adopted, but would eventually become so modified that it was hardly recognisable. The car was shortened, it was modified from two to four doors, and Lord told Burzi to give it a more traditional Austin grille and other family features.

The car emerged at the 1951 Motor Show, billed as the new Austin Seven. It became the A30 Seven soon after, and eventually just the A30. The new model was enthusiastically received by the press and the public but only began to appear in quantity in May 1952, and even then most of the early cars were exported. The home market price was arrived at by the simple expedient of pricing the four-door A30 at £10 less than the two-door Morris Minor.

The A30 proved itself to be extremely economical, and reliable in the best Austin tradition. It was just big enough for four adults, and the luggage space was adequate. But it was a typically cautious Austin design, although at least the Rubicon of unitary construction bodywork was successfully crossed. The A30 was not such an inspired or adventurous design as the Morris Minor had been three years before. Its road

Below This A30 van is likely to have been painted in the prescribed colour scheme for Austin dealers' service vehicles, stone grey and claret red.

Left Introduced in late '53 on the new two-door and revised four-door models, the distinctive combination instrument facia-cum-parcels shelf was reputedly the work of a young apprentice in the Austin styling studio, by the name of David Bache.

Above Under the bonnet of a late-model A30. This first A-series engine is made to look even smaller by the sizeable battery. The vacant shelf next to this was for the heater, still an extra on so many cars even ten years after this photo was taken.

holding and handling were no match for the Minor, the A30 suffering in these respects from the high and narrow proportions dictated by basing the car on the pre-war Austin Seven dimensions.

But Austin was back in the small car market with a vengeance. Two years after the debut of the first A30 a two-door model was added to the range, the much wider doors giving usefully improved access, and at the same time a new facia style was adopted, while boot space was improved by relocating the petrol tank and spare wheel. In the summer of 1954 this was followed by van and estate car versions, the latter, as always with Austin, being known as the Countryman. Both had pressings in the doors and side panels intended to suggest wood trim, but they were of all-steel unitary construction. The van had a roof ventilator, absent on the

Countryman, and this is a telling clue in those not infrequent cases where a van has been modified to Countryman specification with the addition of side windows and rear seat!

A major update for the A30 range followed in 1956. The model was given the newest 948cc version of the A-series engine and a remote-control gearchange, while the body received a wider rear window and a new painted radiator grille – in body colour, with a chrome strip for the surround. Revised gear ratios and a higher final drive meant that the new model was not only faster but also more economical than its predecessor. Two-and four-door saloons, together with van and Countryman models, were offered in this revised A35 range from the start, and there was one extra body style, a real oddity – the A35 pick-up.

This was an amusing miniature

interpretation of the 'coupé utility' theme so much beloved by the Australians, featuring a tail-mounted spare wheel (what Americans would call a 'continental' spare) and with the possibility of seating an additional two passengers in the load area. This last feature and the shortness of the load platform became the model's undoing, as they rendered the vehicle liable to Purchase Tax which made it too expensive. Just under 500 pick-ups were completed, most within months of introduction in late 1956. Almost half were exported, and many were used by Austin dealers as promotional delivery vehicles. They are now highly prized by collectors.

Despite the introduction of the A40 Farina in 1958 the appreciably cheaper A35 models continued in production for a while, but with the coming of the Mini the A35 saloons were discontinued in August 1959. The van and Countryman versions stayed in production and in early 1962 a slightly revised 'Mark II' model was introduced, lacking the indented pressings in the door panels. By now the Mini Countryman was in full production, and only a very small number of the A35 Mark II Countryman model was made before it was discontinued in September 1962. The van still had a long life ahead of it, a

Left A new grille, a bigger rear window and flashing indicators were the external hallmarks of the A35.

Little more than a charming folly, the A35 pick-up sported a rear step and grab rails for anyone adventurous enough to ride in the back, as well as tonneau and spare wheel covers.

Left An authentic A35 (or A30) Countryman can be distinguished from a converted van by the absence of the van's roof ventilator.

Mark III model appearing in the autumn of 1962 fitted with the 1098cc A-series engine. A year later the 848cc unit was offered as an option, and in 1966 the smaller engine was standardized. Production finally ran out in February 1968, but even then there was sufficient demand for a conventional small Austin van to justify an Austin-badged version of the Morris Minor van being brought out to replace the A35.

Not apparently the sportiest of cars, the A30 and A35 models were naturals for economy runs, but they did also appear in other forms of competition. In his early days Graham Hill raced an A35 with a fair degree of success, but it was John Sprinzel who led the gang of A35 racers (before he turned his attention to the Austin-Healey Sprite). Sprinzel and Graham Hill would soon become associated in the Speedwell business, which offered tuning services for the A35 and other BMC vehicles. In much later years the A35 would become a car to be reckoned with in the classic saloon car championship. The A30's moment of glory came with outright victory in the 1956 Tulip Rally, driven by Raymond and Ted Brookes. An A35 was used by a team from the Cambridge University Car Club to put

12,500 mile into a seven-day run at Montlhéry in 1957, establishing seven Class G Records and achieving an overall average speed of 75mph.

Specifications

A30 (SEVEN) 1951-56
Engine four cylinder ohv, 803cc
Bore × stroke 57.9×76.2mm
Power 28bhp @ 4800rpm
Transmission four-speed manual
Chassis unitary construction
Wheelbase 79.5in (2019mm)
Length 136.4in (3464mm) saloon, 137.9in (3502mm) Countryman/van
Width 55.1in (1400mm) saloon, 56in (1422mm) Countryman/van
Height 58.25in (1480mm) saloon, 63in (1600mm) Countryman, 64in (1626mm) van
Weight 1484-1512lbs (674-686kg)
Suspension independent coil front, semi-elliptic leaf rear
Brakes hydraulic
Bodywork four-door saloon, two-door saloon, Countryman, van
Top speed 62mph (100km/h)
Price when introduced £507 (1951 four-door), £476 (1953 two-door), £561 (1954 Countryman)
Total production 84,573 four-door saloons, 88,513 two-door saloons, 29,008 Countrymans and vans, plus approximately 21,170 CKD units

A35 1956-62
As A30, except:
Engine 948cc
Bore × stroke 62.9×76.2mm
Power 34bhp @ 4750rpm
Length 140.5in (3569mm) pick-up
Width 55.1in (1400mm) pick-up
Height 59.25in (1505mm) saloon, 58.75in (1492mm) pick-up
Weight 1512-1568lbs (686-712kg)
Bodywork as A30, with pick-up added
Top speed 73mph (118km/h)
Price when introduced £541 (two-door), £574 (four-door), £639 (Countryman)
Total production 100,284 two-door saloons, 28,961 four-door saloons, 151,652 Countrymans and vans, 475 pick-ups, plus approximately 13,320 CKD units

A35 VAN 'MARK III' (series A-AV8) 1962-68
As A35, except:
Engine 1098cc (1962-66) or 848cc (1963-68)
Bore × stroke 64.6×83.7mm (1098cc), 62.9×68.3mm (848cc)
Power 45bhp @ 5100rpm (1098cc), 34bhp @ 5500rpm (848cc)
Bodywork van only
Top speed 77mph (124km/h) 1098cc model
Price when introduced £388 (basic)
Total production 59,915

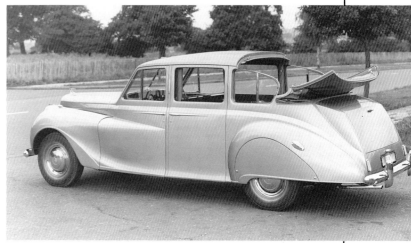

Left As first seen at the 1952 Motor Show, the long wheelbase Princess limousine featured a radiator grille in the original Sheerline/ Princess style.

Below The landaulette was always a rare version. Some were supplied for Royal tours overseas.

Left The long wheelbase saloon model could be supplied with this alternative, 'four-light' elevation and normally did not have a division behind the front seat.

Below This rather special car was a one-off apparently built to special order from the Austin distributor in Spain.

Princess Limousine and Princess IV 1952-1968

The Vanden Plas bodied limousine on the long-wheelbase 4-litre chassis appeared at the 1952 London Motor Show. The styling was taken directly from the short-wheelbase saloon model (described previously) but the limousine body normally had a six-light treatment, and the rear doors were hinged at the rear. Small numbers were also built of a long-wheelbase saloon version with a four-light treatment. The limousine was one of the first new models to be launched after Austin and Nuffield had merged to form BMC, and during the planning stages of the new model some thought was given to producing a Wolseley version. While this was not proceeded with, Vanden Plas models would eventually become available through both Austin and Nuffield dealerships.

The Princess limousine was a very roomy car, capable of seating up to nine people with its folding occasional seats, and it was extremely dignified. Several examples of the model were purchased by the Royal Household over the years, many saw service with British embassies

abroad, and it was a natural choice for the consular or mayoral market. However, most cars were undoubtedly supplied to specialist hire firms including London-based Daimler Hire, and with the chassis being made available to outside coachbuilders for ambulance or hearse bodywork, it was not uncommon to see larger undertakers running a complete fleet of Princess hearses and limousines. In price the Princess usually undercut such competition as was still available, typically the Daimler limousines, and all but established a monopoly of its sector.

With the long-wheelbase limousine

established in production, Austin decided to take a fresh look at the short-wheelbase saloon model, and a new version was introduced in 1956. Originally badged as the Austin A135 Princess IV, its designation was soon shortened to Princess IV, thereby creating a new make at the top of the BMC hierarchy. This was almost an all-new car, with a wheelbase slightly longer than previous short-wheelbase models, a thoroughly re-designed engine, Hydramatic four-speed automatic gearbox, power steering, servo brakes and a new Vanden Plas-designed body.

Above The most familiar version of the Princess limousine, the later model with cut-away rear wheel spats and narrow chrome-plated quarterlight pillar.

Above Hearse chassis were supplied to a variety of specialist coachbuilders, such as Woodall Nicholson of Halifax.

Left The interior of a standard limousine. Several options could be specified for the comfort of rear passengers – a radio, blinds, loose rugs, a footrest and so on. Note the driver's quick-action window lever.

Chauffeur's quarters of a later model limousine. The facia lay-out was very traditional and uninspired, but the woodwork was beautifully executed.

The Princess IV was not in fact a well-proportioned car, looking rather too four-square. It was somewhat expensive, being priced in between the Jaguar Mark VII and the Bentley S-type – an unhappy no-man's land otherwise only frequented by Alvis, Bristol and Lagonda, company in which an Austin cut little ice. The Princess IV was more expensive than the long-wheelbase limousine, and it had the bad fortune to be launched into the post-Suez fuel crisis. In commercial terms the model was not a success, for a mere 200 cars were delivered before production ceased in early 1959.

By then, Kingsbury had taken over the erection of chassis from Longbridge, and in 1960 the limousine models were badged Vanden Plas Princess. The limousine later adopted a single-carburettor detuned version of the redesigned Princess IV engine, and a very mild face-lift was administered, amounting to cut-away spats for the rear wheels and a slimmer chromium-plated pillar between the rear door and the rear quarterlight. Power steering and the automatic gearbox made their appearance on the list of extras, undoubtedly to the great relief of long-suffering chauffeurs.

During the 1960s the model was technically speaking available only to special order, but production figures remained quite steady. Apart from British Royalty, another distinguished customer was the ex-King of Italy, now resident in the USA. A small number of Landaulettes – eighteen in total – were constructed over the years, some being supplied for Royal tours

In production form, hubcaps sported the elegantly written 'P' and a Princess nameplate was found on the front bumper.

Left Originally, the Princess IV (DS7 series) was introduced as the Austin A135 Princess IV, with Flying A mascot and Austin hubcaps.

Below The interior of the Princess IV, as well -finished and luxurious as always. Note the double-width brake pedal on this early automatic-only car. The steering wheel necessarily remained a gigantic affair.

overseas, and a one-off four-light saloon with an altered elevation was built for a Spanish customer. The ambulance and hearse business remained lively, but big custom-made ambulances were gradually phased out by most brigades in favour of smaller and cheaper vehicles built on light commercial chassis, so in the final count the hearses outnumbered the ambulances by almost four to one.

By 1967 there were three limousines still available on the UK market, the Vanden Plas at a competitive £3,259, the Daimler Majestic Major at £3,558 and the Rolls-Royce Phantom V at £10,695. The Vanden Plas and the Daimler were now united in the BMH stable, as BMC and Jaguar, who owned Daimler, had merged in 1966. A new, or at least face-lifted Vanden Plas limousine was under consideration but Jaguar was working on a rather more radical Daimler limousine. It was decided to pool resources, and in consequence the Vanden Plas limousine was dropped altogether, while the Kingsbury factory was given the job of assembling the new Daimler DS420 limousine, which was launched in 1968 and which in scarcely modified form still remained in production at the time of writing. However, with the closure of the old Vanden Plas factory at Kingsbury in

1979 (by then a Jaguar subsidiary) Daimler limousine assembly was brought into the Jaguar factory at Coventry, severing the last link with Vanden Plas coachbuilding tradition.

After more than 20 years, not many Vanden Plas limousines are still earning their keep in the business for which they were designed, but they have a following among collectors with large garages, and have become quite popular in the USA. As certain unscrupulous traders were at one stage in the habit of putting Rolls-Royce radiators on these cars (a practice much frowned upon by Messrs Rolls-Royce) some latter-day purchasers have imagined that they have got a bargain-priced Rolls... and because of confusion with the 4-litre R model it is a popular myth that the limousine model also had a Rolls-Royce engine. Its ancestry was less exalted - the 1939 Austin truck engine, to be precise.

Specifications

PRINCESS LIMOUSINE 1952-68
Engine six cylinder ohv, 3993cc
Bore × stroke 87.3×111.1mm
Power 120bhp @ 4000rpm
Transmission four-speed manual (automatic optional from 1956)
Chassis pressed steel box section

Wheelbase 132in (3353mm)
Length 215in (5461mm)
Width 74.5in (1892mm)
Height 70in (1778mm)
Weight 4810lbs (2184kg)
Suspension independent coil front, semi-elliptic leaf rear
Brakes hydraulic
Bodywork limousine, saloon, landaulette
Top speed 76mph (122km/h)
Price when introduced £2480
Total production 3238 limousines, 88 saloons, 18 landaulettes, plus 774 ambulance/hearse chassis

PRINCESS IV 1956-59
Engine six cylinder ohv, 3993cc
Bore × stroke 87.3×111.1mm
Power 150bhp @ 4100rpm
Transmission four-speed automatic
Chassis pressed steel box section
Wheelbase 121.75in (3092mm)
Length 201in (5105mm)
Width 73in (1854mm)
Height 65.75in (1670mm)
Weight 4480lbs (2034kg)
Suspension independent coil front, semi-elliptic leaf rear
Brakes hydraulic
Bodywork saloon, touring limousine
Top speed 99mph (159km/h)
Price when introduced £3376 (saloon), £3541 (touring limousine)
Total production 178 saloons, 22 touring limousines

Above The Champ in its best-known basic form. Trailers were often towed by Champs in service but the trailer in this factory shot does not appear to be the standard army type.

Right This Champ with sidescreens in place is fully equipped for snorkelling and seems about to be submerged in a tide of mud.

Champ and Gipsy 1952-1968

Sir Alec Issigonis is credited as the man who coined the phrase, "A camel is a horse designed by a committee". He must have been thinking of the Austin Champ, and not without reason.

What eventually became the Champ started out as a wartime project when Whitehall decided that Britain must have its own jeep-type vehicle to replace the American original. Several British car manufacturers were approached and asked to submit designs. It was at this juncture that Austin offered to design a suitable engine, which turned out as the four-cylinder 2.2-litre ohv unit afterwards found in the 1945 Austin Sixteen. But it was the Nuffield design which initially attracted the War Office, and this was a vehicle in which Alec Issigonis had more than a hand. Known unprepossessingly as the 'Gutty' (later the 'Mudlark'), it originally featured unitary all-steel construction, all-round independent suspension with torsion bars, a flat-four engine and of course four-wheel drive. It went through several stages and it was not until 1948 that the final prototype could be turned over to the War Office.

Some Champs were fitted with various types of hard tops; this again is probably a factory experiment.

This was where the committee – also known as the Fighting Vehicles Research and Development Establishment – got its hands on it. They foresaw an active role for the FV1800 as a fighting vehicle, apart from its 'general purpose' functions. They wanted a 90mph machine gun platform as well as substantial off-road capability. There was a decision for all new military vehicles to use the Rolls-Royce FB engine family, with overhead inlet and side exhaust valves, and the FV1800 ended up with the four-cylinder 2.8-litre version of this. A remote five-speed gearbox was fitted,

reverse being totally separate, so in theory the FV1800 could retreat at top speed. The cruciform chassis was now separate from the body, but the independent suspension and the four-wheel drive were retained. A 24-volt electrical system was fitted.

When tenders were issued for car manufacturers to make the FV1800, Nuffield declined with thanks, and instead Len Lord and Austin accepted the contract. This was how the FV1800 became the Austin Champ. Part of the deal was that Austin could make a civilian version powered by their own 2.6-litre engine from the A90 Atlantic

Above The multi-slot grille was typical of the Series I model Gipsy.

Below These days not even the owners' club could muster sufficient Gipsys to rival this massive drive-away at Longbridge, staged in the winter of 1963-64 as part of a publicity boost for the Gipsy Series IV.

Above The original basic Gipsy of 1958 was clearly a Land Rover imitation. Some think it was better-looking, and certainly the fancy wing lines indicate that Austin tried to give their utility vehicle a bit of style.

and Austin-Healey 100, so by a curious twist of fate the engine originally intended for the British jeep did finally end up in the British jeep.

Some 13,000 Champs had been made by 1955. It was not an outstanding success in service. It was a highly sophisticated but therefore also heavy and complicated vehicle, not always reliable, and it was just as well that it had been designed to allow the speedy exchange of major units. It cost the tax payer a lot of money, which led to questions being asked in the House. Even before the last Champs had gone into service the armed forces had begun buying Land Rovers instead, and by the mid-60s the Champs had largely been disposed of as surplus. Production of the civilian Austin-engined model could be measured in hundreds, most such vehicles being exported.

Austin's second stab at a four-wheel drive vehicle was the Gipsy, launched in 1958. This was a more straight-forward exercise, being intended as a rival to the successful Land Rover, which it unashamedly resembled. Oddly enough, the Gipsy again employed all-independent suspension, now with rubber springs and called Flexitor. Another area where it differed from the Land Rover was that it used all-steel rather than aluminium body-

work. This turned out to be a mistake, as the Gipsy thus never had the built-in longevity of its rival. It came with either a petrol or a diesel engine, both being the well-proven Austin 2.2-litre units. The production programme eventually came to parallel the Land Rover range closely, with both short- and long-wheelbase versions, personnel carriers and station wagons, and Austin even did a nice little line in purpose-built factory equipped fire tenders, with water tanks, pumps and hose reels.

The Gipsy would never become a serious threat to the Land Rover. It was never considered for military use, but some civilian fleet buyers and other authorities did acquire at least small numbers of Gipsys, presumably to try out the newcomer. Most of them quickly reverted to the well-proven Land Rovers. Substantial numbers of Gipsys were however purchased by the Civil Defence authority, and many of these were still being kept in the proverbial mothballs in the early 1990s, in readiness for whatever calamity might befall the nation.

Later models of the Gipsy came to be even more Land Rover-like, especially when the Flexitor suspension was discarded in favour of good old-fashioned beam axles and semi-elliptic leaf springs. There was a rear

wheel drive only version with a pick-up body. Production was moved from Longbridge to BMC's commercial vehicle factory at Adderley Park in East Birmingham, the old Wolseley and Morris-Commercial plant. After introduction of the Series IV models in 1962 the Gipsy continued to trickle off the production lines in insignificant numbers. When the BMC-Leyland merger brought Austin and Rover into the same fold in 1968, the Gipsy was one of the first casualties, superfluous to requirements.

Austin never considered a Gipsy replacement, but an offshoot of the Mini-Moke programme had been a rather fearsome twin-engined, four wheel drive version, and later the ADO19 Ant project came close to production. This used an 1100 transverse powerpack with clever additional gearing to transmit power also to the rear wheels. It could have given the company a 15-20 year lead over the Japanese, who were to exploit small four wheel drive recreational vehicles in the 1980s, but it was another casualty of the BMC-Leyland merger, reputedly being given the thumbs down by the Land Rover engineers!

Above Austin supplied the Gipsy fire tenders quite as fully equipped as indicated by this picture, taken outside the engineering block at Longbridge.

Above The later Gipsys such as this Series IV model of 1961 had a two-part wiremesh grille, the lower part being removeable to permit installation of a winch.

Now that they have pedestrianised Birmingham's Corporation Street you can no longer park your Gipsy outside The Midland Educational while you dash into Rackham's. In any case a long-wheelbase Gipsy hardly seems the ideal city centre shopping vehicle for madame, notwithstanding the fancy hubcaps and wheeltrims.

Specifications

CHAMP (civilian model) 1952-55
Engine four cylinder ohv, 2660cc
Bore × stroke 87.4×111.1mm
Power 75bhp @ 3750rpm
Transmission five-speed manual, separate reverse, four-wheel drive
Chassis box section cruciform semi-integral with body
Wheelbase 84in (2134mm)
Length 144.5in (3670mm)
Width 61.5in (1562mm)
Height 71.5in (1816mm)
Weight 3470lbs (1575kg)
Suspension independent with torsion bars front and rear
Brakes hydraulic
Bodywork open four-seater utility
Top speed 65mph (105km/h)
Price when introduced £950 (basic)
Total production approx 1200

CHAMP (military model) 1952-55
As civilian model, except:
Engine four cylinder inlet over exhaust, 2828cc
Bore × stroke 88.9×114.3mm
Power 80bhp @ 3750rpm

Weight 3668lbs (1665kg)
Price when introduced £1100 (basic)
Total production approx 11,700

GIPSY s.w.b. petrol engine 1958-68
Engine four cylinder ohv, 2199cc
Bore × stroke 79.4×111.1mm
Power 62bhp @ 4100rpm (later models 72bhp @ 4000rpm)
Transmission four-speed manual, separate high/low transfer box, four-wheel drive (later models, optional rear wheel drive only)
Chassis box and tubular section
Wheelbase 90in (2286mm)
Length 139in (3531mm), later models 142.9in (3629mm)
Width 66.75in (1695mm)
Height 73.5in (1867mm), later models 74.75in (1899mm)
Weight 2688-2860lbs (1220-1298kg)
Suspension independent with Flexitor rubber elements front and rear, later semi-elliptic leaf springs front and rear
Brakes hydraulic
Bodywork three-seater open utility with soft or hard top, pick-up truck, fire tender

Price when introduced £650 (basic)
Total production all Gipsys 1958-68, 21,208

GIPSY s.w.b. Diesel engine 1958-68
As petrol model, except:
Engine four cylinder ohv Diesel, 2178cc
Bore × stroke 82.6×101.6mm
Power 55bhp @ 3500rpm
Weight 2820-3000lbs (1280-1362kg)
Price when introduced £755 (basic)

GIPSY l.w.b. petrol or Diesel engines 1960-68
As s.w.b. models, except:
Wheelbase 111in (2819mm)
Length 160in (4064mm), later models 163.9in (4162mm)
Weight 2890-3147lbs (1312-1429kg)
Suspension independent with Flexitor rubber elements front, semi-elliptic leaf springs rear, later models semi-elliptic leaf springs front and rear
Bodywork as s.w.b., also personnel carrier
Price when introduced £720 petrol, £830 Diesel (basic prices)

The original Healey 100 before the 1952 Motor Show, with Austin-type disc wheels, and the windscreen reclined.

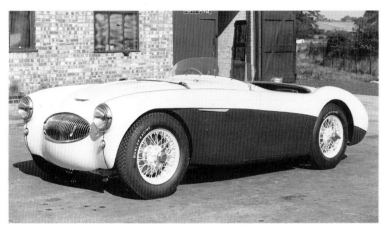

Austin-Healey 100, 100-Six and 3000 1952-1968

It is quite possible that the improvised marriage between Austin and Healey effected at the 1952 Motor Show was not so hastily arranged as it seemed to contemporary observers. A marriage of convenience it certainly was, for both parties. For Donald Healey and his tiny, stagnating sports car company at Warwick, it was a chance for fame and fortune; for the Austin company, it was the lure of having a sports car with which to compete against MG in the American market.

The Healey 100 prototype was duly introduced in production in 1953 as the Austin-Healey 100. It used many standard Austin components, including the 2.6-litre engine from the A90 Atlantic, but also the gearbox, rear axle, suspension and steering came from the Longbridge parts bin. The body was styled by the Healey people, specifically Gerry Coker, and was to prove a particularly timeless design, being but little modified during the fifteen-year production life of the Big Healey. The complete body/chassis unit, with part aluminium, part steel panelling, was manufactured by Jensen at West Bromwich (who had

previously supplied Austin with the A40 Sports bodies).

The new model was an almost instant success in the USA. The Healey company was paid a royalty on every car built, and the factory at Warwick became in effect an adjunct to the BMC development and competitions departments, as well as a sales outlet. The Austin-Healey began to make a name for itself in racing, and a special tuning kit was developed at Warwick. This was fitted to the 100 'M' model of 1955-56, by which time the basic car had also benefitted from a four-speed gearbox in place of the original three-speeder. Overdrive was always a standard fitment. Then there was the rather fiercer 100 'S' model, of which some fifty cars were built at Warwick in 1955, with an even more modified engine and all-aluminium bodywork. This was only available in one standard colour scheme, white over blue, chosen as they were the official racing colours of the USA.

Unfortunately, continued use of the old big four engine was proscribed under BMC's new rationalisation policy. The Austin-Healey was redesigned and emerged in 1956 as the 100-Six, fitted with the new C-series six-cylinder 2.6-litre unit. The bodywork was also modified, with two occasional

Above left The 100 'S' model looked superficially like an ordinary 100 but had no bumpers and only this low perspex windscreen. Under the skin the differences were substantial.

Above The 100 was a particularly pleasing design with simple and uncluttered lines. This shows the windscreen in the normal upright position. The tonneau cover was standard on this model.

Austin-Healey 100 interior featured bucket seats and full instrumentation. Odd position of gearlever was because gearbox had been designed for A70/A90 column change.

Below The 2.6-litre engine with two SU carburettors was from the Atlantic.

Above As originally installed in the 100-Six model, the BMC C-series engine had an inlet manifold integral with the cylinder head which rather restricted output.

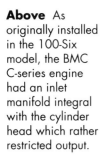

Left The 'M' model with the tuned, Le Mans-type engine had a louvred bonnet with a leather strap across it. Many were finished in two-tone colour schemes.

Left Under the bonnet of a 100 'S' was this much-tuned engine with the carburettors on the 'wrong' side compared to the standard model.

Right The 100-Six four-seater was offered in this 'basic' version with disc wheels and no overdrive.

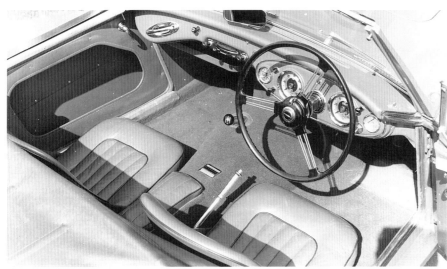

Left This style of interior was common to the 100-Six and 3000 models until the Mark III Convertible model appeared in 1963.

seats being carved into the rear tonneau. A basic model fitted with disc wheels and lacking overdrive was made available. The performance of the original 100-Six was not impressive, as the cylinder head with a cast-in inlet manifold restricted breathing rather severely. A year later a new cylinder head with a separate manifold was fitted which greatly improved matters.

Also in 1957 Austin-Healey production was moved from Longbridge to the MG factory at Abingdon, and in 1958 a two-seater version of the 100-Six was introduced. In 1959, the 100-Six was replaced by the 3000, which was available in both two- and four-seater form from the start. The original 3000 Mark I models were difficult to distinguish from the 100-Sixes externally, but the enlarged 2.9-litre engine and front disc brakes were valuable improvements. Right from the start, the 3000 proved itself an excellent rally car, fast but rugged if occasionally hampered by its notorious lack of ground clearance. In 1960 Pat Moss won the Liège-Rome-Liège rally in a 3000, a victory repeated by Rauno Aaltonen in 1964, while the Morley brothers won the 1961 and 1962 Alpine Rallies.

A 3000 Mark II followed in 1961, with a three-carburettor engine, but

this proved to be a short-lived experiment and in 1962 the twin-carburettor engine was reintroduced on the 3000 Convertible. This had wind-up windows instead of loose sidescreens, and a much-improved hood. The Convertible was only available in four-seater form, and the old two- and four-seater models were soon discontinued. In late 1963 the 3000 Mark III model was introduced, with bigger carburettors and the engine now developing 148bhp. The Mark III also had an improved interior with a wooden facia, although Ambla

Above The two-seater version of the 100-Six had a much deeper tonneau panel.

Left Most exciting (and rarest) of the 3000 engines was the triple-carb version, found on the Mark II two- and four-seater models of 1961-62.

trim was now standard in place of leather. During the run of the Mark II a new gearbox had been introduced, with a centre-mounted change instead of the always slightly awkward side-mounted gearlever of the earlier cars. In 1964 came the last fundamental improvement: a new rear axle and suspension incorporating radius arms, which assisted handling and gave a bit more ground clearance at the back.

The vast majority of Big Healeys were always sold in the USA, and when it was realised that the car would not meet the new American safety and

The 3000 Mark I had shared its wavy-line grille with the 100-Six but the Mark II model was treated to a new, vertical-bar grille.

Below The same grille was found on the Mark III model, here in its final 'Phase II' form with separate flashing indicators. The Convertibles had a new windscreen, wind-down windows with quarterlights, and a more substantial hood.

The Mark III interior was more civilised, with a wood facia and centre console, although the seats were now upholstered in Ambla rather than leather.

emissions standards to be introduced from 1 January 1968, BMC decided to discontinue the model, although the production line was kept busy almost to the end with large orders still coming in from American distributors. The final car – which was a one-off home market model – was built in early 1968. The Healey family had produced the prototype for a replacement, the 4000, with a widened body and the Rolls-Royce engine from the Vanden Plas Princess 4 litre R, but this found little favour with top BMC management and even less with the Leyland people who were moving in after the BMC-Leyland merger in early 1968. At one stage BMC had toyed with the idea of producing an Austin-Healey version of the new MGC, but this was sensibly vetoed by Donald Healey. And so the Big Healey line came to an end after only fifteen years, leaving the Sprite model to carry on the name for a short while.

Left The 1961 Alpine Rally saw a famous Healey victory for the Morley brothers. However, this is Peter Riley's car; he was less fortunate, crashing after the brakes failed.

Another time, another place. In 1957 Austin-Healey assembly was moved from Longbridge to the MG factory at Abingdon. The 100-Sixes and Sprites shared assembly lines with the MGA models.

Specifications

AUSTIN-HEALEY 100 1952-56
Engine four cylinder ohv, 2660cc
Bore × stroke 87.3×111.1mm
Power 90bhp @ 4000rpm
Transmission three-speed manual with overdrive (four-speed on BN2 model from 1955)
Chassis pressed steel box section
Wheelbase 90in (2286mm)
Length 151in (3835mm)
Width 60.5in (1537mm)
Height 49in (1245mm)
Weight 2150lbs (976kg)
Suspension independent coil front, semi-elliptic leaf rear
Brakes hydraulic
Bodywork open two-seater
Top speed 103mph (166km/h)
Price when introduced £1064
Total production 14,634 (of which 4604 BN2 models including 100M)

AUSTIN-HEALEY 100 'S' 1955
As Austin-Healey 100, except:
Power 132bhp @ 4700rpm
Transmission four-speed manual, no overdrive
Length 148in (3759mm)
Height 42in (1067mm)
Weight 1924lbs (873kg)
Brakes hydraulic, discs front and rear
Top speed 119mph (192km/h)
Price when introduced US$4995 (£1784) – UK list price not quoted
Total production 55

AUSTIN-HEALEY 100 'M' 1955-56
As Austin-Healey 100 (BN2 model), except:
Power 110bhp @ 4500rpm
Weight 2168lbs (984kg)
Top speed 109mph (175km/h)
Price when introduced £1212
Total production 640 factory-built (and a further 519 cars converted from standard specification by Healeys at Warwick)

AUSTIN-HEALEY 100-SIX 1956-59
Engine six cylinder ohv, 2639cc
Bore × stroke 79.4×88.9mm
Power 102bhp @ 4600rpm (early cars), 117bhp @ 4750rpm (later cars)
Transmission four-speed manual (overdrive optional)
Chassis pressed steel box section
Wheelbase 92in (2337mm)
Length 157.5in (4001mm)
Width 60.5in (1537mm)
Height 49in (1245mm)
Weight 2435lbs (1105kg)
Suspension independent coil front, semi-elliptic leaf rear
Brakes hydraulic
Bodywork open four-seater, two-seater from 1958
Top speed 103mph (166km/h) early cars, 111mph (179km/h) later cars
Price when introduced £1144 (four-seater), £1227 (two-seater)
Total production 11,294 four-seaters, 4150 two-seaters

AUSTIN-HEALEY 3000 MARK I 1959-61
As 100-Six, except:
Engine 2912cc
Bore × stroke 83.3×88.9mm
Power 124bhp @ 4600rpm
Brakes hydraulic, discs at front
Top speed 114mph (183km/h)
Price when introduced £1168 (two-seater), £1176 (four-seater)
Total production 10,825 four-seaters, 2825 two-seaters

AUSTIN-HEALEY 3000 MARK II 1961-63
As 3000 Mark I, except:
Power 132bhp (convertible model 131bhp) @ 4750rpm
Weight 2460lbs (1117kg) convertible model
Bodywork open four-seater and two-seater (1961-62), convertible (1962-63)
Top speed 112mph (180km/h), convertible model 117mph (188km/h)
Price when introduced convertible model £1190
Total production 5096 four-seaters, 355 two-seaters, 6113 convertibles

AUSTIN-HEALEY 3000 MARK III 1963-68
As 3000 Mark II Convertible, except:
Power 150bhp @ 5250rpm
Weight 2548lbs (1157kg)
Bodywork convertible only
Top speed 121mph (195km/h)
Price when introduced £1107
Total production 17,712

The original 1200cc 1954 Metropolitan had this rather heavy grille design and a bonnet air scoop. Whitewall tyres and radio aerial were typical, and colour schemes as yet monotone.

Alternative to the convertible model was this hard top, with a triple-split panoramic rear window. Most 'Metros' had the Nash nameplates, but some were also badged Hudson.

Metropolitan 1954-1961

An eminent historian once described the Metropolitan as 'a motoring cuckoo'. An exotic bird of strange parents it certainly was, yet the metaphor falters as this cuckoo did not push its foster-siblings from the nest – in the end it was the Metropolitan which got the push.

The American Nash company (which later merged with Hudson to form American Motors) was a pioneer of the compact car, having introduced the Rambler in 1951. It was developing a design for an even smaller two-seater car, at first scheduled to incorporate Fiat mechanical components. Its styling was typical of Nash, with partly enclosed wheels and all the grace of a soapdish. Then of all people Donald Healey (who had worked with Nash on the Nash-Healey sports car) introduced Nash president George Mason to Len Lord of Austin. The outcome was an agreement whereby the NX1 – soon re-named Metropolitan – would be built in Birmingham, incorporating Austin mechanical components. Fisher & Ludlow of Castle Bromwich – a BMC subsidiary from 1952 onwards – made the body, and final assembly was undertaken by Austin. The exclusive

A typical Metropolitan interior, with part cloth, part vynide trim, in a black and silver grey colour combination regardless of exterior colour.

marketing rights were held by Nash.

The Metropolitan was launched in the USA and Canada in early 1954. It was certainly a 'new' type of car, combining the dimensions and economy of European models with the styling and some of the fitments of domestic American models. Basically a two-seater – with childrens' seats behind – it was available in convertible or hardtop forms. At first the engine was the 1200cc unit from the Austin A40, but in 1956 a change was made to the new 1489cc BMC B-series engine. A three-speed gearbox sufficed

for American tastes, with a steering-column change of course. Suspension, steering and brake systems were borrowed from the A40 or A30 models. The boot was only accessible from inside the car, but a 'continental' spare wheel was stuck on the tail. Two-tone colour schemes were almost *de rigueur*, a heater and a radio were fitted as standard, and whitewall tyres were a popular option.

The Metropolitan did surprisingly well, enjoying the distinction together with the MGA of being the best-selling British-made car in the USA until then.

Metropolitan bodies were made by
Fisher & Ludlow at Castle Bromwich – the
war-time Spitfire factory which is now
Jaguar's body plant.

A quayside of Metropolitans awaiting
shipment to the USA; but why are some
of them crated and others not?

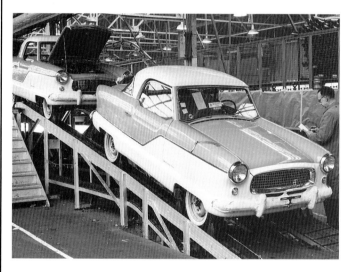

Coming off the elevated assembly line in
Longbridge's CAB 1, these Metropolitans
are the later 1500 models with mesh
grille and typical two-tone split.

The Metropolitan was released for home
market consumption in early 1957. The
sign in front of the car may say 'Austin'
but the car never wore the Austin badge,
only the bold 'M' seen on the hubcaps.

It was sometimes sold as a brand in its own right, sometimes as a Nash or a Hudson. One suspects that it found particular favour with women buyers. More surprisingly it was adopted by some American police forces for traffic warden duties replacing three-wheeled Harley Davidsons. What passed for an instruction book was a joke, surely even by undemanding American standards.

In 1957 Austin obtained the agreement of American Motors to sell the Metropolitan through Austin outlets in Britain and in those foreign markets where American Motors did not trade. The result was the Metropolitan 1500, which was only sporadically called an Austin and never wore the Austin badge. The appearance of right-hand drive Metropolitans in the home market was greeted with polite puzzlement by the press. Ever praiseworthy of the British industry's successes in the important American export market, the magazines could not quite make up their minds why the Metropolitan had to be inflicted on British buyers. As always, a totally non-sporting two-seater caused bewilderment. The mechanical specification of the 'Austin' version was unchanged, the performance failed to impress, and thanks to its short wheelbase and narrow track the Metropolitan lurched rather than handled. But it was a novelty, it was considered smart in some fashionable circles of the day, and it was certainly different. It found a niche in Britain, some European markets and South Africa.

Then in 1959 the big three US car makers introduced their first compacts, which soon reduced American Motors to one of the also-rans in the small car stakes. Sales of imported European cars suffered badly, even more so when recession hit the USA in 1960, reducing all car sales. It was a suitable opportunity for American Motors to pull the plug on the Metropolitan and extricate themselves from the agreement with BMC. Only recently had a fourth series Metropolitan been introduced, with an opening boot lid, and small numbers continued to be made both for the American and for

Two factory demonstrators pose for the lens in a Cotswold village. These left-hand drive cars may be North American export models but could also be destined for European markets, where the Metropolitan was sold through the Austin network.

Last of the line, the Series IV model of 1960-61 boasted quarterlights to the door windows and an external opening bootlid.

other markets into 1961. Some of the last ones took a long time to sell.

American Motors afterwards concentrated on their bigger compact car models, including the Rambler American and Rambler Classic series. There was no direct successor to the Metropolitan although perhaps a distant echo of the original theme might be found in the new generation of two-seater 'not quite sports' cars spearheaded by Ford's Mustang in 1964. The Austin company was happy to pocket its Dollars – the Metropolitan had been an immensely profitable exercise for the company – but had no thoughts for a Metropolitan successor either. From 1962 onwards, BMC's marketing effort in North America was concentrated mainly on sports and performance cars.

Specifications

METROPOLITAN 1200 1954-56
Engine four cylinder ohv, 1200cc
Bore × stroke 65.5×88.9mm
Power 42bhp @ 4500rpm
Transmission three-speed manual
Chassis unitary construction
Wheelbase 85in (2159mm)
Length 149.4in (3794mm)
Width 61.5in (1562mm)
Height 54.4in (1381mm)
Weight 1869lbs (849kg)
Suspension independent coil front, semi-elliptic leaf rear
Brakes hydraulic
Bodywork convertible, hard top
Top speed 73mph (117km/h)
Price when introduced convertible US$1469 (£524), hard top US$1445 (£516)
Total production 5004 convertibles, 15,003 hard tops

METROPOLITAN 1500 1956-61
As Metropolitan 1200, except:
Engine 1489cc
Bore × stroke 73×88.9mm
Power 52bhp @ 4500rpm
Length 149.5in (3797mm)
Height 56in (1422mm) hard top, 56.5in (1435mm) convertible
Weight 1885lbs (856kg) hard top, 1876lbs (852kg) convertible
Top speed 75mph (121km/h)
Price when introduced (UK launch in 1957) hard top £714, convertible £725
Total production for Nash/Hudson 14,395 convertibles and 60,566 hard tops, approx 9400 for UK and other markets

The new Cambridge had almost revolutionary styling by previous Austin standards. It still wore the 'flying A' and the 'Austin of England' script but had a new badge on the bonnet.

From the Cambridge launch presentation in the exhibition hall at Longbridge in 1954.

A40, A50 and A55 Cambridge 1954-1958

By 1954 the rotund styling of the Somerset/Hereford generation was beginning to look distinctly dowdy and behind the times against the competition from Ford, Hillman or Vauxhall – some of whose offerings in the family car class had, ironically, been introduced earlier than the Austins. The in-house rival, Morris, a partner with Austin in BMC since 1952, had a new family saloon, the Oxford Series II, ready for launch in the spring of 1954, using (as might be expected) the new Austin-BMC B-series engine of 1½ litres. The 1954 Motor Show saw the debut of a new Austin family car range, which revived the name of Cambridge. Some might have considered Longbridge's choice of the rival university town as a riposte to Cowley, but in fact the name of Cambridge had first been used for the Austin Ten in 1936.

The mechanical components were based on well-tried Austin practice. The A40 version of the new car had a 1200cc version of the new B-series engine, in many respects redesigned compared to the Devon/Somerset engine, but the A50 had the new 1489cc engine. Where the Morris and other Nuffield cars with these engines used SU carburettors and electric fuel pumps, the Austins stuck to Zenith carburettors and mechanical fuel pumps. The clutch was given hydraulic actuation, and the four-speed gearbox had improved baulk-ring synchromesh but was still controlled by a column change. The cam and lever steering, coil and wishbone i.f.s. and hydraulic brakes did not present any surprises to students of Austin design.

However, the body was all new. Following on from the A30, Austin now introduced unitary construction for the bigger models in the range too. The wheelbase was longer by almost 7in than it had been on the Somerset, which greatly improved rear seat access and accommodation. The boot was also usefully larger and more sensibly shaped, with the spare wheel in a tray below. The styling was almost radical by Austin standards. The inspiration was to a degree still American, but now several generations ahead, being full width with completely integrated wings, a low and wide radiator grille – the first on an Austin to feature the 'crinkled' horizontal bars – and a very Oldsmobile-like 'cow-hip' feature line along the sides of the body.

The interior was more like a spaceship than an old-school Austin, with the metal facia panel curving away, chrome-plated slides for the

Right Another view of the Cambridge presentation, featuring a couple of the almost non-existing two-door models.

Below The engine compartment of a prototype Cambridge, not exactly well filled.

heater controls, and the instruments – including a quadrant type speed-ometer – in a binnacle above the steering column. While the new car was still the work of Austin's own styling department under Dick Burzi, none other than Mrs Kay Petre was employed as a consultant for the interior design and the colour schemes.

It was originally the intention to launch two- and four-door versions of the Cambridge models, but very few two-door cars were made and none ever reached the general public. Both the A40 and A50 were available in standard as well as de-luxe forms, the latter versions featuring leather upholstery, more chrome plating and slightly better equipment. Although Austin toyed with the idea of a Cambridge estate car, nothing ever came of this. The old, Devon-type commercial derivatives soldiered on into 1956 with the new Cambridge 1200cc engines, but in that year Austin brought out a new ½-ton van and pick-up featuring the Cambridge styling and the 1½-litre engine. These derivatives were to have a long life indeed, being still offered in 1971, with Morris badge-engineered versions becoming available in 1962, at the same time as the ½-ton models were facelifted with a new grille, and in the following year the

1622cc B-series engine was fitted. They were the basis for all sorts of special bodies, ranging from motor-homes to hearses.

In late 1956 the Cambridge was given 13in wheels in place of the original 15in wheels, and the A50 compression ratio was raised, marginally increasing engine output. It was however only in February 1957 that the model received a facelift to bring it into line with the contemporary six-cylinder models. This was more in the nature of a tail-lift as the changes only affected the rear end, which became 5in longer, with a deeper bootlid and the rear lights relocated in modest fins. The rear window was larger, and a chrome trim strip was added to the side of the car, giving Austin's designers a chance to introduce some fancy two-tone colour schemes. The revised model was known as the A55. The 1200cc engine option was dropped, except for CKD cars assembled in Eire, where the new smaller-engined model was known as the A45.

In the last few months of production the A50 had been offered with the options of either overdrive or

Here the Austin photographer has captured the rare two-door Cambridge on test in a Welsh setting.

Manumatic two-pedal drive, whereby the clutch was activated by movement of the gearlever. These options were continued on the A55, which also became available with a floor-mounted gearlever. Production continued into 1958 but was allowed to run down in the autumn of that year in preparation for the launch of the new Farina-styled A55 Cambridge Mark II.

The mid-50s Cambridges were by no means outstanding and had no pretensions to performance, with top speeds around 70-75mph, but with these cars Austin brought its mid-range family saloon model thoroughly up-to-date. The Cambridges were effective contenders in a popular sector of the market and their sales far outstripped their Morris cousins. It may be mentioned that the Cambridge also found a ready welcome in Japan, where the model was assembled by Nissan, as the Somerset had been before it.

In early 1957 the Cambridge became the A55 model, with a completely re-designed rear end and a wider rear window. Additional chrome trim and two-tone colour schemes were part of the package, but the front end was not changed.

The Cambridge-based ½-ton van replaced the Devon-based commercials in 1956.

The facia was as revolutionary by Austin standards as the exterior. The badge on the horn push of the steering wheel was the coat of arms adopted by Lord Austin in 1936.

A 1961 example of the ½-ton pick-up, one of the last before the face-lift.

How the ½-ton range ended up after the 1962 face-lift. This example is actually one of the Morris-badged versions, introduced in that year. The Austins retained the typical wavy-line bars in the new full-width radiator grille.

Specifications

A50 CAMBRIDGE 1954-57
Engine four cylinder ohv, 1489cc
Bore × stroke 73×88.9mm
Power 50bhp @ 4400rpm
Transmission four-speed manual (overdrive or Manumatic optional from 1956)
Chassis unitary construction
Wheelbase 99.25in (2521mm)
Length 162.25in (4121mm)
Width 61.5in (1562mm)
Height 61.5in (1562mm)
Weight 2248lbs (1021kg)
Suspension independent coil front, semi-elliptic leaf rear
Brakes hydraulic
Bodywork two-door saloon (prototypes only), four-door saloon
Top speed 74mph (119km/h)
Price when introduced £678 (standard), £721 (de luxe)
Total production 114,867 (including ½-ton van and pick-up)

A40 CAMBRIDGE 1954-56
As A50 Cambridge, except:
Engine 1200cc
Bore × stroke 65.5×88.9mm
Power 42bhp @ 4500rpm
Price when introduced £664 (standard), £707 (de luxe)
Total production 30,666

A55 CAMBRIDGE 1957-58
As A50 Cambridge, except:
Power 51bhp @ 4250rpm
Length 167in (4242mm)
Weight 2352lbs (1068kg)
Top speed 77mph (124km/h)
Price when introduced £808
Total production approx 154,000 (including ½-ton van and pick-up)

½-TON VAN/PICK-UP 1956-63
As A50 Cambridge, except:
Power 47bhp @ 4100rpm
Transmission four-speed manual
Length 168.75in (4286mm)
Width 62.5in (1588mm)
Height van 68.75in (1746mm), pick-up 63.25in (1607mm)
Weight 2212lbs (1004kg)
Bodywork van, pick-up, chassis/cab, chassis/scuttle
Price when introduced £577
Total production approx 124,000 (to 1971) and approx 26,000 Morrises

½-TON VAN/PICK-UP 1963-71
As 1956-63 model, except:
Engine 1622cc
Bore × stroke 76.2×88.9mm
Power 56bhp @ 4500rpm
Weight van 2253lbs (1023kg), pick-up 2246lbs (1020kg)
Total production see 1956-63 model

Austin's first popular medium-sized six after the war was the A90 Westminster, with styling following on from the Cambridge.

... and all that jazz. The A105 was Austin's vision of a luxury-sporting compact, 1956-style. The only item of period decoration missing on this car would be an external sun visor!

A90 and A95 Westminster and A105 1954-1959

Launched virtually at the same time as the Cambridge models, the A90 Six Westminster bore a very obvious family resemblance to the new A40/A50 but in its way represented an even bigger step forward for Austin. The styling was the same, although only the doors were interchangeable with the Cambridge, as the Westminster was built 2½in wider and had a longer front end to accommodate its new six-cylinder engine. With the Westminster Austin turned its back on the out-of-date big four-cylinder engine and followed the lead of Ford and Vauxhall by providing a fairly compact family saloon with the combination of refinement and high performance that a six-cylinder engine can give.

The new BMC C-series engine was a direct development of the B-series, with the same basic layout as the four and sharing its 88.9mm stroke; however, with a bigger bore (79.4mm as opposed to 73mm) capacity was 2,639cc, usefully greater than the contemporary 2¼-litre engines available from Ford and Vauxhall. Design and manufacture of the C-series engine

The new 2.6 litre C-series engine was quite a lump but there was still plenty of room under the A90 Westminster's bonnet.

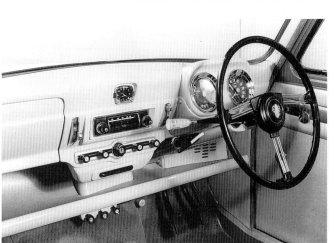

The interior was also Cambridge-like but the Westminster driver had two round dials to look at.

Left The A105 had this almost-Austin-Healey engine with two SU carburettors. The heater and windscreen washer were standard fittings on this model.

Above The roofrack was standard on the Countryman and two-tone colour finishes were common, but this example also sports a radio, whitewall tyres and wheel trims from an A105.

For 1957 the Westminster became the A95 model, with a new grille and a new, longer rear end. The two-tone split was also different, with extra chrome trim strips.

was undertaken by Morris Engines at Coventry, and the new unit also became available in Morris and Wolseley models in the winter of 1954-55. In the Westminster, with a 7.3:1 compression ratio and a single Zenith carburettor, the engine developed some 85bhp, sufficient it seems for Austin to claim the 'A90' epithet for the car, to which they at first added the 'Six' in an effort to avoid confusion with the Atlantic, now safely dead and buried. 'Westminster' was another old Austin name revived; the original Westminster had been a compact four-light saloon body on a six-cylinder 16hp chassis in 1931. The new A90 Westminster proved to be capable of a genuine 85mph, giving it a 4mph advantage over Ford's Zephyr Six or Vauxhall's Velox.

We need not dwell on the Westminster's specification in detail, which was mostly just like the Cambridge. Being wider, the car was roomier, and was as close to a real six-seater as was ever offered by Austin. Interior appointments were again similar to the Cambridge but instruments were circular, and the de-luxe Westminster had four separate armrests for the front seats, and two-tone colour schemes for its leather upholstery. An overdrive was optional.

In the spring of 1956 the additional A105 model was introduced. It had a high-compression engine with two SU carburettors and developed 102bhp, virtually identical to the Austin-Healey 100-Six engine. The suspension was lowered and the A105 was dressed up with all the right trimmings, including fog lamps, wheel trims, whitewall tyres and two-tone colour schemes. This was a 95mph car and an effective rival for the Ford Zodiac and Vauxhall Cresta. The original A105 lasted only a matter of months, however, as a restyled Westminster was shown at the 1956 Motor Show, emerging as the A95. This had a slightly more powerful high-compression engine, a new radiator grille, and a longer tail with the rear lamps mounted in fins. Two-tone colour schemes spread to the A95, which usually had a contrast-colour flash with chrome mouldings along the side of the car. The A105 version of the revised model had the same stylistic updating, with engine unchanged but overdrive now fitted as standard. Both A95 and A105 were now offered with a Borg-Warner automatic gearbox as an option. There was an alternative body, available only with the A95 specification, in the form of an all-steel four-door estate car, and as was traditional for Austin it was

known as the Countryman.

For those customers desiring greater luxury and exclusivity Austin offered an up-market alternative in 1958 in the shape of the A105 Vanden Plas. These started life as ordinary A105s on the Longbridge assembly lines, but were dispatched without interior trim to Vanden Plas at Kingsbury in London, to be kitted out with luxurious leather trim and walnut door cappings and facia. Only 500 were made of this precursor to the Princess 3 litre. Another unusual version of the Westminster, probably made in even smaller numbers, was confined to Australia, where A95 saloon and Countryman models were assembled from CKD kits and re-badged as Morris Marshalls, with different radiator grille and chrome mouldings. Production of the A95 and A105 continued through most of 1959, the cars being replaced in the autumn of that year by the new A99 Westminster.

Unlike most previous Austins of the postwar period, the Westminster in its various forms was quite an effective performer and was one of the models selected as 'promising' when the BMC Competitions Department was established in 1955. The A90 and the A105 were rallied spasmodically over the next three years but without achieving

Left The Vanden Plas treatment, or what Kingsbury did to the interior of an A105. The deeply recessed instruments became a Vanden Plas hallmark. Most of these cars probably had the automatic gearbox. The dished steering wheel with half horn ring arrived with the 1956 facelift.

The facelifted A105 could now mainly be distinguished from the A95 by its fancy wheel trims and extra driving lamps.

any outstanding performances. An A90 was one of five BMC cars, alleged to be standard production models, which in 1955 put more than 100 miles into one hour each at Montlhéry, John Gott completing all but 102 miles during his hour at the wheel of the Westminster. Successes were achieved in saloon car racing by drivers such as Ken Wharton and Jack Sears, who won the first annual British Saloon Car Championship with his A105 in 1958.

A different sort of achievement was that of Richard Pape, war-hero and writer, who in 1955 drove an A90 from North Cape at the top of Norway to Cape Town in South Africa, the first time this trip had been accomplished. Pape's first A90 crashed in Norway but the substitute, hurriedly provided by the Austin agents in Oslo, survived the gruelling journey across two continents.

Specifications

A90 SIX WESTMINSTER 1954-56
Engine six cylinder ohv, 2639cc
Bore × stroke 79.4×88.9mm
Power 85bhp @ 4000rpm
Transmission four-speed manual (overdrive optional)
Chassis unitary construction
Wheelbase 103.75in (2635mm)
Length 170.25in (4324mm)
Width 64in (1626mm)
Height 63.75in (1619mm)
Weight 2912lbs (1322kg)
Suspension independent coil front, semi-elliptic leaf rear
Brakes hydraulic
Bodywork four-door saloon
Top speed 86mph (138km/h)
Price when introduced £792 (standard), £834 (de luxe)
Total production 25,532

A105 SIX 1956
As A90 Six Westminster, except:
Power 102bhp @ 4600rpm
Height 62.5in (1588mm)
Top speed 96mph (155km/h)
Price when introduced £1109
Total production approx 1000

A95 WESTMINSTER 1956-59
As A90 Six Westminster, except:
Power 92bhp @ 4500rpm
Transmission four-speed manual (overdrive or automatic optional)
Wheelbase 105.75in (2686mm)
Length 180.75in (4591mm)
Height 62in (1575mm)
Weight 2996lbs (1360kg)
Bodywork four-door saloon, Countryman
Top speed 91mph (146km/h)
Price when introduced £999 (saloon), £1216 (Countryman)
Total production 28,065

A105 1956-59
As A95 Westminster, except:
Power 102bhp @ 4600rpm
Transmission four-speed manual with overdrive (automatic optional)
Weight 3024lbs (1373kg)
Bodywork four-door saloon
Top speed 96mph (155km/h)
Price when introduced £1200
Total production approx 5270

A105 VANDEN PLAS 1958-59
As A105, except:
Weight 3105lbs (1410kg)
Top speed 94mph (151km/h)
Price when introduced £1474
Total production 500

The happily-smiling Frog-eye Sprite became a great favourite with women buyers. Most cars had the front bumper but it was technically an extra, not included in the list price.

Right One reason why this Sprite was so cheap to make was that it had no external boot lid, but this was one of its less popular features.

Austin-Healey Sprite 1958-1971

With the Big Healey successfully established, Len Lord conceived the idea for a small, cheap sports car – a modern version of the old MG Midget, in a sector of the market that MG themselves had only recently vacated. He took the idea to Donald Healey, and Donald briefed his son Geoffrey. A funny little car began to take shape in the Warwick development shop in 1956. Its unitary body was designed to be cheap and simple to make, and the mechanical components came from the small BMC saloon cars: A-series engine, Austin A35 front suspension and Morris Minor rack-and-pinion steering. The quarter-elliptic rear suspension and the brakes were specially developed.

The Sprite was instantly accepted by Len Lord and George Harriman when they saw the prototype in 1957. When the new car was launched in 1958, it also won instant acceptance from the press and public alike. Almost by coincidence the Sprite had acquired a happily smiling face, with prominent frog-eye headlamps in pods on the bonnet, and most people found it totally endearing. In standard form it

was very basic but the list price was only £669, which brought sports car motoring within reach of a new sector of the public. With its slightly tuned twin-carburettor engine the Sprite's performance had the edge over the small saloons then available, and it was a responsive little car, a pleasure to drive.

Tremendously successful though the Frogeye Sprite was, it was not without its shortcomings. There was no external bootlid, and the one-piece front end, which incorporated bonnet and wings, was awkward to lift. There were also those who did not care for the froggy-eyed face. These aspects were therefore addressed in the development of the Mark II model, which appeared in 1961. Although the centre section and underbody of the

car were unchanged, as was largely the mechanical specification, new front and rear ends gave the Mark II Sprite an almost totally new look, styled to give the car a family resemblance to the new MGB. There was a conventional top-opening bonnet, the headlamps were mounted in the wings, and there was an opening boot lid flanked by small tailfins with vertical lamp units. BMC took the opportunity to bring out a badge-engineered version of the Sprite, reviving the MG Midget name. This pleased MG dealers and traditional MG buyers but deprived the Healeys of royalty payments on the MG-badged cars, which would eventually oust the Sprite altogether.

The Mark II Sprite was a much-improved car but it would soon meet

Above The interior was as simple as the exterior, with vynide upholstery and rubber mats on the floor. This car is fitted with at least three extras – the rev. counter, the windscreen washer and the heater.

Above With the entire front end lifting up in one piece, access was quite difficult to the rear of the engine compartment, so the battery was often overlooked.

Left More convenient but less colourful: the Sprite Mark II of 1961.

head-on competition from the new Triumph Spitfire. In response to Triumph BMC fitted the Sprite with a bigger 1098cc engine in 1962, and from then the race was on, the two rival companies always trying to get the better of one another. A Mark III version of the Sprite followed in 1964, having an improved version of the 1098cc engine, semi-elliptic rear springs, wind-down windows and a new facia. Two years later the Mark IV followed, with a 1275cc engine and a much more civilized convertible-type hood instead of the old pack-away item. And in late 1967 cars destined for the American market received the first emissions-control engine, dual-circuit brakes and a rather ugly padded facia.

However, time was running out for the Sprite. In 1968 BMC introduced the 1300-based Austin America saloon in the US market, and decided henceforward to badge all sports cars as MGs in North America. This meant that the Sprite was from then on available only in the home market. The 1970 models received the first facelift after the BMC-Leyland merger and appeared with Rostyle wheels, black sills and radiator grille, and revised badging. There was now only the nameplate to signify the difference between Sprite and Midget. At the end of 1970 British Leyland boss

The Sprite Mark III of 1964 featured wind-down windows and external door handles, and wire wheels were now an optional extra.

Donald Stokes cancelled the contract to use the Healey name, so from January 1971 there was a 'new' model in the range, known as the Austin Sprite. This was a meaningless charade, with only about 1000 home market cars being sold before the Sprite was finally discontinued in the middle of the year, leaving the MG Midget to continue until 1979.

Although the Sprites with their small-capacity engines were rarely in the running for overall wins, they were extremely competitive in their class, in rallying as well as racing. One of the most famous Sprite drivers was John Sprinzel, who also gave his name to a

much-modified Frogeye. His Sprite was third overall in the 1960 Liège-Rome-Liège and second in the 1960 RAC Rally, with class wins on both occasions. Sprites also did very well in the Sebring races, scoring a number of class wins from 1959 onwards, and a much-modified Sprite won its class in the 1960 Le Mans 24-hour race. Later racing Sprites had very aerodynamic coupé bodies which helped one such car to win its class at Le Mans in 1965, coming 12th overall. In another inventive bit of BMC badge-engineering, the old MG record breaker EX.179 reappeared as an 'Austin-Healey Sprite' EX.219 in 1959. Fitted with a 948cc

Below A new facia design was introduced on the Mark III and continued to the end of Sprite production.

Right Sprite Mark IV with the optional-extra hard top, the last in a series of different hard top designs.

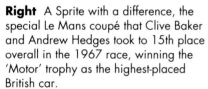

Right A Sprite with a difference, the special Le Mans coupé that Clive Baker and Andrew Hedges took to 15th place overall in the 1967 race, winning the 'Motor' trophy as the highest-placed British car.

Above The post-Leyland facelifted Sprite had these Rostyle wheels, blacked-out sills and a new blacked-out grille, as well as a new seat design. Less obvious is the fact that this is a 1971 Austin Sprite, made after the Healey name had been dropped.

Sprite engine, it set a number of international class G records at speeds up to 147mph.

A Sprite with a difference was produced by BMC licensee Innocenti in Italy, who fitted Sprite mechanical components into their own pretty Ghia-designed body from 1960 onwards. This model was produced in small numbers until 1970 and largely followed the up-dates of the British car, although it was never fitted with the 1275cc engine. It was appreciably more expensive than the Sprite in those markets where the two cars sold against each other.

Specifications

SPRITE MARK I 1958-61
Engine four cylinder ohv, 948cc
Bore × stroke 62.9×76.2mm
Power 43bhp @ 5200rpm
Transmission four-speed manual
Chassis unitary construction
Wheelbase 80in (2032mm)
Length 139.5in (3543mm)
Width 53in (1346mm)
Height 49.75in (1264mm)
Weight 1466lbs (666kg)
Suspension independent coil front, quarter-elliptic leaf rear
Brakes hydraulic
Bodywork open two-seater

Top speed 83mph (134km/h)
Price when introduced £669
Total production 48,987

SPRITE MARK II 1961-62
As Sprite Mark I, except:
Power 46.5bhp @ 5500rpm
Length 136in (3454mm)
Weight 1566lbs (711kg)
Top speed 85mph (137km/h)
Price when introduced £641 (standard), £656 (de luxe)
Total production 20,450

SPRITE MARK II 1098cc 1962-64
As Sprite Mark II, except:
Engine 1098cc
Bore × stroke 64.6×83.7mm
Power 56bhp @ 5750rpm
Brakes hydraulic, discs at front
Top speed 88mph (142km/h)
Price when introduced £668
Total production 11,215

SPRITE MARK III 1964-66
As Sprite Mark II 1098cc, except:
Power 59bhp @ 5750rpm

Length 137.4in (3489mm)
Width 54.9in (1394mm)
Height 48.5in (1232mm)
Weight 1530lbs (695kg)
Suspension independent coil front, semi-elliptic leaf rear
Top speed 92mph (148km/h)
Price when introduced £611
Total production 25,905

SPRITE MARK IV 1966-71
As Sprite Mark III, except:
Engine 1275cc
Bore × stroke 70.6×81.3mm
Power 64bhp @ 5800rpm
Height 48.6in (1235mm)
Weight 1575lbs (715kg) 1966-69, 1632lbs (741kg) 1969-71
Top speed 94mph (151km/h) 1966-68, 96mph (154km/h) 1968-71
Price when introduced £672 (Austin Sprite, January 1971, £924)
Total production 20,357 (H-AN9 model 1966-69), 1411 (H-AN10 model, 1969-70), 1022 (Austin Sprite A-AN10 model, 1971)

Left Externally, the A40 Farina was a radical departure from convention, whether Austin's or anybody else's, but under the skin it stuck to utterly traditional solutions.

Left The 1961 Mark II had a longer wheel-base, more rear legroom, and a new grille.

Above The interior was quite basic on the early cars, and carried over the instrument pack from the A35.

A40 Farina 1958-1967

However well the Austin company had been served by Dick Burzi's consider-able talent over the years, there was perhaps a feeling that for the future a different approach would be required. The decision after the BMC merger to go for a policy of sharing bodyshells between different marques – the policy that became known as badge-engineering – afforded the possibility of a fresh start in design. A new style was needed, a new style which broke away from the traditions of either Austin or Morris. In 1955 Len Lord and his second-in-command George Harriman decided to go shopping in Turin. They settled for the services of Pininfarina, the most outstanding Italian designer, and thus began a ten-year relationship.

The first project entrusted to the Italian designer was the replacement for the A35. The mock-up which arrived at Longbridge in 1956 was quite remarkably like the production model introduced two years later, the main difference being that the very slim roof pillars of the original were substantially thickened to strengthen the body structure. Not only was the new A40 a complete departure from all previous Austin designs, it was also a milestone

in automotive design as such, being the first modern two-box car without an extended boot at the back. The general theme as well as the detail of the styling followed Farina's then prevalent thinking, with crisp and simple lines akin to those of the Lancia Flaminia.

The underpinnings, however, were fairly directly derived from the A35, as were the mechanical components, with the 948cc engine in a similar state of tune and suspension, steering and braking systems all very similar too. Unfortunately this meant that the A40 had the odd hydro-mechanical rear brakes from the A35. The original facia was rather austere and used the A35 instrument pack. The A40 was wider and had a longer wheelbase, and was a great improvement on the older car in terms of roominess. The two long doors made it much easier to get into and out of; there was never any consideration of a four-door A40 Farina (which would have looked very strange indeed!).

The new model was extremely well received at its launch in the autumn of 1958. The A35 saloon models continued in production for almost another year, in fact until Longbridge began to turn out the first Minis, so the A40 was not quite the A35 replacement that it had been intended to be. An additional A40

variant was introduced in 1959, Austin taking the logical step suggested by the shape of the A40 to make a Countryman version with a two-piece horizontally split tailgate and a folding rear seat – the first small hatchback saloon car.

Fair numbers of the A40 models were sold abroad, even in North American markets, and the car was assembled in several overseas factories including Australia. In 1959 BMC concluded an agreement with the Innocenti company of Milan for Innocenti to manufacture selected BMC models under licence, the first of which was to be the A40 in both saloon and Countryman versions. The Innocenti A40 was introduced at the 1960 Turin Motor Show, and more than 67,000 of these cars were made up to 1967, with the Italian version being updated along with the British car.

In 1961 a Mark II version of the A40 Farina was introduced. The wheelbase was increased by 4in, which improved rear seat room, but dimensions were otherwise unchanged. There was a new full-width radiator grille with horizontal bars which no longer had the crinkly Austin look. The engine was fitted with an SU rather than a Zenith carburettor, there was a new and more substantial looking facia, and the simple counter-balanced drop

Arguably the first modern hatchback, this 1959 version of the A40 was called the Countryman in the best Austin tradition. The elegantly-dressed young woman is Cecilia Overthrow, who worked in Austin's publicity department and allegedly owned the poodle.

Below Under the Mark II bonnet, where an SU carburettor replaced Austin's traditional Zenith.

windows in the doors were replaced by proper winding windows. The rear brakes were given fully hydraulic actuation. In the following year the model was further improved, with the new 1098cc version of the A-series engine and baulk-ring synchromesh in the gearbox. Little further in the way of modification was done to the car, except for a simplified radiator grille in 1963 and a mock woodgrain facia in 1964. With the Mini selling in ever increasing numbers and the 1100 heading for the number one position in the UK sales chart, the A40 was clearly on borrowed time after 1963, and output and sales were falling from year to year. Nevertheless it survived right through to November 1967 and so almost made it into the Leyland era. The car that in 1958 had heralded a new age for Austin ended up as the last conventional small rear wheel drive car to bear the name.

The A40 Farina had its moment of glory, too. Pat Moss and Ann Wisdom used A40s to win the Coupe des Dames two years running, 1959 and 1960, in the Monte Carlo rally. Their 1959 mount, a very early A40 registered XOE 778, was rediscovered and restored some 20 years later, and in the hands of Paul Skilleter resumed its career, now in historic rallying, finishing up as

overall winner of the 1985 Coronation rally. In its day the A40 could also give a good account of itself in saloon car racing, the most prominent practitioner being Dr George Shepherd, whose much-modified A40 attracted a great deal of attention in 1959 and 1960, regularly winning the under 1000cc class and finishing as the overall champion in 1960.

The final facia on the Mark II was finished in what they used to call Yugoslav ironwood, while the instrument pack was common to the new Morris 1100.

Specifications

A40 FARINA MARK I 1958-61
Engine four cylinder ohv, 948cc
Bore × stroke 62.9×76.2mm
Power 34bhp @ 4670rpm
Transmission four-speed manual
Chassis unitary construction
Wheelbase 83.5in (2121mm)
Length 144.25in (3664mm)
Width 59.4in (1508mm)
Height 57.25in (1454mm)
Weight 1680lbs (763kg)
Suspension independent coil front, semi-elliptic leaf rear
Brakes hydraulic
Bodywork two-door saloon, Countryman
Top speed 72mph (116km/h)
Price when introduced £676 (basic saloon), £689 (de-luxe saloon), £660 (Countryman)
Total production 141,899 saloons, 27,713 Countrymans

A40 FARINA MARK II 1961-62
As Mark I, except:
Power 37bhp @ 5000rpm
Wheelbase 87.1in (2211mm)
Weight 1800lbs (817kg)
Top speed 75mph (121km/h)
Price when introduced £657 (basic saloon), £694 (de-luxe saloon), £679 (Countryman), £716 (Countryman de-luxe)
Total production 35,133 saloons, 14,744 Countrymans

A40 FARINA MARK II 1098cc 1962-67
As Mark II, except:
Engine 1098cc
Bore × stroke 64.6×83.7mm
Power 48bhp @ 5100rpm
Top speed 79mph (127km/h)
Price when introduced £619 (saloon), £640 (Countryman)
Total production 80,605 saloons, 42,086 Countrymans

Big for a 1½-litre car, the Farina Cambridge and its derivatives always gave the feeling of being somewhat over-bodied. Perhaps there was too much overhang all round. The tailfins were controversial at the time.

A55 Mark II and A60 Cambridge 1959-1969

After the A40 Farina, it was only a matter of time before the other Austin models would receive the attention of the Italian master stylist. But where the A40 Farina was and remained unique to the Austin marque, subsequent Farina designs all appeared in several different guises, bearing anything up to six different badges in line with the badge-engineering philosophy now warmly embraced by BMC. The next new Austin was therefore launched first as a Wolseley, the 15/60, which appeared most unseasonably a few weeks after the 1958 Motor Show. The Austin version was launched in January 1959 and was followed over the next few months by Morris, MG and Riley models all based on the same common design.

The new A55 Mark II Cambridge and its companions were, in aesthetic terms, not quite as successful as the A40 Farina. They were rather large for 1½-litre family saloons, being almost 15ft in length, and the very pronounced tailfins were a subject of controversy. It is not known whether Pininfarina sketched out the new Cambridge on a bad day, or whether

his original proposals were altered in the Longbridge styling studio, but it is instructive to compare the Farina Cambridge to the Farina-designed Peugeot 404, which followed the same general style and which was first introduced in 1960.

The A55's wheelbase was the same as on the superseded Cambridge and the track only fractionally wider, so the new car gave the impression of being somewhat overbodied. There was not

Austin's bold new frontage, or the Farina treatment applied to the Cambridge. The 'flying A' did survive on the first-generation Farina styled models but in a highly stylized form.

The A60 version had those tailfins somewhat trimmed, with a new grille and contrast-colour sideflashes also providing a stylistic update.

really any more interior room than on the old model although the boot offered rather more space. However it is still a bit of a shock to open the bonnet of a Farina Cambridge and see all that wasted space between the radiator and the grille, and it is interesting that BMC Australia were able to insert a 2.4-litre six-cylinder engine in the same bodyshell without major modification to create the unique Austin Freeway. The 1489cc engine was carried over from the previous Cambridge, except that Austin engineers now threw caution to the wind and fitted an SU carburettor. Most of the A55 Mark II cars had the floor change but a column change was still offered, and together with a one-piece bench seat remained quite popular in many export markets. Suspension, steering and brakes all followed Austin practice.

The new Cambridge was a perfectly honest motorcar and was quite capable of holding its own in the marketplace. It was certainly a fairly painless transition for Austin devotees into a new era, and thanks to the very visible tailfins it was a delightfully easy car to manoeuver. But it was not terribly inspired, and alongside the new generation of front-wheel drive Austins it looked increasingly old-fashioned. Nevertheless there was always a clientele who preferred the 'traditional' type of Austin – after they got used to the Italianate styling of the new offering – and the Cambridge family continued to do very well indeed for BMC, notching up more than 850,000 sales between them from 1959 to 1971.

A Countryman estate car version followed the Cambridge saloon in 1960, and in the autumn of 1961, when most of the BMC models received a facelift, the Cambridge was updated and emerged as the A60. This had a modified radiator grille, a new facia, and slightly cut back tailfins. Under the bonnet was a 1622cc engine, and the new model could be supplied with the Borg-Warner type 35 automatic gearbox.

For conventional cars (as opposed to Issigonis's packaging masterpieces) the Farina Cambridges were quite roomy. This A60 still features a steering-column gearchange, but most had the classic floor change.

The opportunity was taken to fractionally increase the wheelbase and track dimensions, which improved the handling of the car as well as rear seat room. The Countryman version of the A60 shared the new saloon's mechanical specification and interior but retained the original body styling with the soaring fins.

In the following year, the Cambridges and their Morris Oxford Series VI cousins were offered with a diesel version of the B-series engine. This

The original tailfin design was carried over from the A55 to the A60 Countryman. How do we know that this is an A60? Simple, it has the A60 style facia.

retained the old capacity of 1489cc and had primarily been developed for use in the corporation's light commercial vehicles. The result was not quite Britain's first diesel-engined passenger car in series production – Standard had offered a diesel Vanguard in 1954 – and frankly did not have a great deal of impact. The B-series diesel engine was no paragon of smoothness and performance was lacklustre – top speed of the diesel Cambridge was around 66mph compared with 81mph of the petrol-engined model, and acceleration suffered equally. Most of the diesel models were sold for export to countries where different excise duties made diesel cars an attractive proposition in financial terms, and many undoubtedly saw use as taxicabs.

As the 1960s wore on the Cambridges and their relatives became an unobtrusive part of Britain's street furniture. Somehow the model established itself as a more prestigious offering in the 1½-litre class than contemporary Fords, Hillmans and Vauxhalls. Although the company car market in the UK had not yet achieved the massive proportions it would later reach, the Cambridge was much beloved by fleet operators, who were inclined to fight shy of BMC's front-wheel drive offerings with their patchy reliability

record. In an unusually rational move by BMC production planners, assembly of the Cambridge was eventually moved to the Morris factory at Cowley where all other versions of the design were put together, leaving Longbridge free to concentrate on front-wheel drive cars. The Cambridge was finally discontinued in 1969 (its Morris and Wolseley counterparts were kept going for another two years). It was supposedly replaced by the Austin Maxi, but was it really?

Specifications

A55 CAMBRIDGE MARK II 1959-61
Engine four cylinder ohv, 1489cc
Bore × stroke 73×88.9mm
Power 52bhp @ 4350rpm
Transmission four-speed manual
Chassis unitary construction
Wheelbase 99.25in (2521mm)
Length 178in (4521mm)
Width 63.5in (1613mm)
Height 59.75in (1518mm)
Weight 2473lbs (1123kg)
Suspension independent coil front, semi-elliptic leaf rear
Brakes hydraulic
Bodywork four-door saloon, Countryman
Top speed 78mph (126km/h)
Price when introduced £801 (saloon), £915 (Countryman)
Total production 142,000 (approx) saloons, 7994 Countrymans

A60 CAMBRIDGE 1961-69
As A55 Cambridge Mark II, except:
Engine 1622cc
Bore × stroke 76.2×88.9mm
Power 61bhp @ 4500rpm
Transmission four-speed manual (automatic optional)
Wheelbase 100.25in (2546mm)
Length 174.5in (4432mm)
Top speed 81mph (130km/h)
Price when introduced £854 (saloon), £978 (Countryman)
Total production 229,000 (approx) saloons, 36,184 Countrymans (including Diesel Countrymans)

A60 CAMBRIDGE DIESEL 1962-69
As A60 Cambridge, except:
Engine 1489cc Diesel
Bore × stroke 73×88.9mm
Power 40bhp @ 4000rpm
Transmission manual only
Weight 2520lbs (1144kg)
Top speed 66mph (106km/h)
Price when introduced £823 (saloon), £931 (Countryman)
Total production 11,350 (approx) saloons (Countrymans included in petrol Countryman figure above)

The better-proportioned A99 Westminster was a handsomer car than the Cambridge, but the basic styling theme was exactly the same.

A99 and A110 Westminster 1959-1968

Hot on the heels of the Farina-designed A40 and A55 models, the new Westminster followed in July 1959. Although the styling followed the themes of the A55 Cambridge and thus presented no surprises whatsoever, the more generous proportions of the larger car gave the A99 Westminster an altogether more pleasing appearance, and the tailfins were not quite so prominent as on the smaller car. The result was a well-proportioned if rather ponderous car, somehow possessed of a dignity which put it at a level well above the flashy and insubstantial Ford and Vauxhall models. Indeed, the new Austin aspired more towards the Rover-Humber end of the market.

This tendency was strengthened by the presence under the bonnet of a bored out 3-litre version of BMC's C-series engine complete with two SU carburettors –not quite but almost the engine that had recently been introduced in the Austin-Healey 3000. It was coupled to a novel and intriguing gearbox, a three-speeder with Porsche-developed synchromesh on all forward ratios and fitted as standard with an overdrive on second

The one that got away: the only prototype of the Vanden Plas-trimmed luxury version of the Westminster, tentatively dubbed the A120 model.

The interior of the new Westminster was rather basic and could have done with the wood-and-leather treatment to disguise some of that painted metal. Note the two-tone trim and the overdrive switch under the parcels shelf.

and top. This gave the driver a total of five speeds to play with, controlled from a column change but with the overdrive control tucked away under the parcels shelf. First gear was on the high side, which occasioned some complaints. A fully automatic Borg Warner gearbox was available as an optional extra.

Suspension and steering followed the practice of the previous Westminster, but there was an important innovation in the braking department, as the A99 had Lockheed front disc brakes with servo assistance. It was the first BMC saloon car to use disc brakes and, outside the sports and prestige car class, one of the first British family saloons so equipped.

The most disappointing feature of the Westminster was undoubtedly its interior: a very plain painted metal facia and some not-quite U two-tone colour combinations for the trim, which was not even leather on the standard model. However, BMC had a well-defined hierarchy, and those in search of a luxury version of the same car could always opt for the better-equipped Wolseley 6/99. There were no plans for Morris or Riley versions of the new six-cylinder car, nor an MG either, but it was the intention to introduce specially trimmed Vanden

Plas versions of the new big Austin and Wolseley. These came very close to reality, with a few pre-production examples being made, and early Westminster literature made mention of the car, which was to be known as the A120. It would have a slightly more powerful engine, a totally retrimmed wood and leather interior on the same lines as the superseded A105 Vanden Plas, additional lamps and extra chrome trim. However, there was a quick re-think and the A120 was dropped. Instead BMC brought out the Princess 3-litre, described elsewhere.

There were no body variations of the A99 although at least one Countryman was built, which rendered sterling service as a tender car to the BMC Competitions Department's rally team. No time was wasted in trying to make a competitions car out of the Westminster, and the appearance of one of these cars in the 1962 Monte Carlo rally was motivated by publicity – Robert Glenton from the Sunday Express being in the crew. He crashed the car. End of Westminster competition career.

At the time of the great BMC re-vamp of 1961, the Westminster became the A110. The engine was unchanged in size but a new twin exhaust system resulted in a few more bhp. There was

In 1961 the Westminster became the A110 model, with a more powerful engine and this new radiator grille.

a new and rather more attractive radiator grille, the facia and interior trim were improved, and an additional two inches in the wheelbase gave more rear seat room. The gearlever was moved to the floor but the three-speed plus dual overdrive gearbox was still fitted, although Westminsters supplied to the Constabulary regularly had four speed gearboxes, incidentally of the 'side-change' type found on the Austin-Healey 3000. The automatic option was still available, and power-assisted steering could now also be supplied, as could air conditioning.

The last type of Westminster appeared in 1964, under the title of A110 Mark II. The major mechanical change was the introduction of a four-speed gearbox, the same type as found on the later Austin-Healey 3000 cars with floor-mounted 'centre change', and overdrive was now an option. The Mark II also had smaller 13in wheels as opposed to the earlier cars' 14in wheels. Two models were offered, a standard and a super-de-luxe. The standard model had an unattractive mesh grille and vinyl upholstery. The super-de-luxe had the horizontal bar

The still-more powerful A110 Mark II of 1964, externally unchanged from its predecessor.

This Police version of the A110 Mark II is the rare standard model with the mesh grille. Posing outside the 'Kremlin' administration block at Longbridge, this is probably a factory demonstrator rather than an actual police car.

The A110 Mark II super-de-luxe was much more luxurious than previous Westminsters, but was inflicted with a rather down-market strip speedometer. The floor change controlled a new four-speed gearbox.

grille of the previous A110, leather upholstery, reclining seat backs with picnic tables for the rear seat passengers, and a wooden facia and door cappings. In 1965-66 there was a short-lived interim de-luxe model which dispensed with the wood trim and picnic tables but was otherwise similar to the super-de-luxe. All of the Mark II models had an unfortunate rectangular instrument pack with a strip speedometer which seemed to have been borrowed from the 1100/1800 models, and which sat rather uneasily on a traditional wooden facia.

Like the Cambridge, the Westminster was one of those Austin models whose production was moved to Cowley, joining the equivalent Wolseley and Vanden Plas Princess models. Production of these cars gradually dwindled to insignificant figures, and the last Westminsters were made in January 1968, a few months after the replacement Austin 3 litre had been introduced. The Westminster was a comfortable large family car with a good turn of speed, being capable of 100mph, but it was a type of car left behind by the developments of the 1960s.

Specifications

A99 WESTMINSTER 1959-61
Engine six cylinder ohv, 2912cc
Bore × stroke 83.3×88.9mm
Power 103bhp @ 4500rpm
Transmission three-speed manual with overdrive (automatic optional)
Chassis unitary construction
Wheelbase 108in (2743mm)
Length 188in (4775mm)
Width 68.5in (1740mm)
Height 59in (1499mm)
Weight 3305lbs (1500kg)
Suspension independent coil front, semi-elliptic leaf rear
Brakes hydraulic, discs at front
Bodywork four-door saloon
Top speed 98mph (158km/h)
Price when introduced £1148
Total production 15,162

A110 WESTMINSTER 1961-64
As A99 Westminster, except:
Power 120bhp @ 4750rpm
Wheelbase 110in (2794mm)
Height 60.5in (1537mm)
Weight 3470lbs (1575kg)
Top speed 102mph (164km/h)
Price when introduced £1270
Total production approx 12,200

A110 WESTMINSTER MARK II 1964-68
As A110 Westminster, except:
Transmission four-speed manual (overdrive or automatic optional)
Price when introduced £999 (standard), £1113 (super de-luxe)
Total production approx 13,900

Kind hearts may be more than coronets, but it was the coronet which was adopted as the radiator badge for the new Vanden Plas marque. The original 1959 3 litre may have been an exercise in badge-engineering but it was an appealing car all the same.

Surely a real chauffeur would have doffed his cap to the young lady? Apart from badging, the 3 litre could be distinguished from the rear by the extravagant overriders.

It was the interior of the Princess 3 litre which set it apart from its BMC cousins of lesser breeds. On cars with automatic gearbox such as this, the inconvenient switch under the parcels shelf was an intermediate speed hold.

Vanden Plas Princess 3 litre and 4 litre R 1959-1968

The original intention had been to launch Vanden Plas-trimmed versions of the new Farina-styled Austin Westminster and Wolseley 6/99 cars of 1959, but there was a quick change of mind within BMC's marketing department, and instead the new Princess 3 litre made its bow at the 1959 London Motor Show. From the side the new model could be mistaken for either of its siblings, but there was a new radiator grille at the front, a truncated version of that found on the big Princess 4 litre limousine, and more elaborate rear bumpers. The interior trim was quite up to Vanden Plas standards, with a wooden facia in fair imitation of Rolls-Royce, and sumptuous leather upholstery, as well as picnic tables and other niceties.

The advantage of badging the car as a Princess was that the model could be sold without prejudice through either the Austin or the Nuffield dealer network, although in those export markets where the split franchise system still persisted it was normally exclusive to the Austin dealers. In the BMC hierarchy the Princess was somewhat above Wolseley, and this was reflected in the price. For the first year the car was known just by its model name, but in 1960 BMC conveniently invented Vanden Plas as a make in its own right. Nameplates were discreetly confined to the rear of the car, only a small coronet being carried on the radiator grille surround.

In mechanical terms the 3 litre did not differ greatly from the Austin and Wolseley models, but it is likely that a greater proportion of the Princess cars had fully automatic transmission and were fitted with power steering when this became available in 1962. Only a limited range of fairly dignified colour schemes, including some restrained two-tone combinations, were available. The Princess 3 litre cars were produced in the Cowley factory, and were only sent to the Vanden Plas factory at Kingsbury in London to receive their final trim; some cars were even completed at Cowley.

The 4 litre R model created a great deal of interest in 1964 but never lived up to the expectations of the sales department. From this angle, the repositioned fog lamps indicate that this is the new model rather than a 3 litre.

Below This is apparently the actual Princess Countryman supplied to HM The Queen. Another half dozen similar cars were supplied to favoured customers.

A 3 litre Mark II was launched in the autumn of 1961, following the lead of the Westminster by adopting a floor-mounted gearchange on the manual gearbox model. It came with a twin exhaust system and a slightly more powerful engine. This continued in production for another three years. Although the saloon was the only catalogued model, some half-dozen estate cars were specially made by Vanden Plas, of which one was supplied to HM The Queen, two to Leonard Lord and George Harriman respectively, and the remainder to a few selected large Austin distributors.

There was a school of thought within BMC which felt that the corporation should produce an even bigger and more exclusive prestige car to cover the upper echelons of the market and to compete with the Jaguar Mark X and Rover 3 litre. A contact was established with Rolls-Royce who, it transpired, were having one of their periodic bouts of soul-searching: should they make a smaller car than their normal Silver Cloud/S-type? The upshot was that a sort of joint venture was undertaken, for a car based on the big BMC Farina bodyshell and fitted with a Rolls-Royce engine. The chosen engine was a four-litre unit, type FB.60, with overhead inlet and side exhaust valves for its six cylinders. This was part of a Rolls-Royce engine family which dated back to the 1940s, with four-, six- and eight-cylinder versions. These engines had mostly been used in military vehicles, among them the Austin Champ, but the big straight-eight had seen service in the Rolls-Royce Phantom IV.

The Rolls-Royce (or Bentley) version of the car remained stillborn, although it is likely that the experiment proved useful to Rolls-Royce in the development of the unitary construction Silver Shadow. The BMC car was introduced with some fanfare in 1964, unhandily titled the Vanden Plas Princess 4 litre R. Compared to the original Princess 3 litre the rear end of the body was restyled, with new horizontal tail lights and the roofline raised to give more headroom in the rear seat. Automatic transmission and power steering were standard. The new car cost just under

Differences at the rear were more extensive, with new rear wings, boot lid and horizontally arranged rear light clusters. The styling was somehow not as satisfying as the original, being rather messy and dominated by the long-winded model name.

Below The interior of the 4 litre R was well up to the standard expected of a Vanden Plas model, although by now the Westminsters and Wolseleys were almost equally luxurious.

Specifications

VANDEN PLAS PRINCESS 3 LITRE MARK I
1959-61
Engine six cylinder ohv, 2912cc
Bore × stroke 83.3×88.9mm
Power 103bhp @ 4500rpm
Transmission three-speed manual with overdrive (automatic optional)
Chassis unitary construction
Wheelbase 108in (2743mm)
Length 188in (4775mm)
Width 68.5in (1740mm)
Height 59in (1499mm)
Weight 3465lbs (1573kg)
Suspension independent coil front, semi-elliptic leaf rear
Brakes hydraulic, discs at front
Bodywork four-door saloon
Top speed 97mph (156km/h)
Price when introduced £1397
Total production 4715

VANDEN PLAS PRINCESS 3 LITRE MARK II
1961-64
As 3 litre Mark I, except:
Power 120bhp @ 4750rpm
Wheelbase 110in (2794mm)
Height 60.5in (1537mm)
Weight 3660lbs (1662kg)
Top speed 105mph (169km/h)
Price when introduced £1532
Total production 7900

VANDEN PLAS PRINCESS 4 LITRE R 1964-68
As 3 litre Mark II, except:
Engine six cylinder inlet over exhaust, 3909cc
Bore × stroke 95.3×91.4mm
Power 175bhp @ 4800rpm
Transmission automatic only
Height 59in (1499mm)
Weight 3530lbs (1603kg)
Top speed 106mph (171km/h)
Price when introduced £1995
Total production 6999

£2000, the tax-break limit on company cars. It performed well if not outstandingly with a 107mph top speed, but was rather thirsty. Handling was indifferent, with strong understeer, and sadly the engine was not quite so refined as the public had been led to believe by all the publicity, which put a great deal of stress on the Rolls-Royce connection.

This was another car for which BMC set too optimistic production targets. Talk of a hundred cars per week soon proved to be so much hot air, and the total run of the model was only some 7000 cars before production ceased in 1968. Some of them took a very long time to shift, too, with several 'new' examples having been in stock for up to two years. It had been BMC's intention to put the car into production in their new Southern Rhodesian

assembly plant at Umtali, but Ian Smith came along with U.D.I. and the Wilson government promptly severed all trading links with Rhodesia. For many years, Umtali was a costly white elephant for BMC; officially it was their property, but they were unable to exercise any control over it and the company never had any return on the considerable investment.

The 4 litre R could have been so much better a car, especially if the proposed Rolls-Royce twin overhead cam engine had gone into series production. Still, with the BMC-Jaguar merger in 1966 the Jaguar Mark X became an adopted son of the house, and there was no longer any need for BMC to offer a competitor.

Great man, great idea, small car. Alec Issigonis shows off the compact powerplant of the Mini at the press launch in 1959.

Seven and Mini 1959-1969

1959 was BMC's annus mirabilis. The company had an almost completely new range of cars in the most popular classes. The Leonard Lord inspired policy of rationalisation by badge engineering had been successfully introduced, and the new Farina-styled designs had brought Austin and the other BMC marques into a new era. In the twelve months to August 1959 ten new car models had been launched. And the best was yet to come. On 26 August 1959 BMC launched the Austin Se7en (sic) and the Morris Mini-Minor, two revolutionary small cars that turned the motoring world completely upside down.

The story of the conception and birth of the Mini is well known. Alec Issigonis, designer of the Morris Minor, latterly working for the Alvis company, was tempted back to BMC by Len Lord and in 1956 joined Austin at Longbridge. After the impact of the Suez crisis and the short-lived bubble car boom, Lord asked him to design a 'proper' small car. In what now seems an incredibly short space of time Issigonis and a few assistants had the basic Mini prototype ready. He took Len Lord for a five-minute drive round

the factory, and Lord immediately decided that this car must go into production within a year.

For some time Issigonis had been a believer in front wheel drive. In order to get the existing BMC A-series engine to fit into the smallest possible four-seater car, his masterstroke was to turn the engine sideways and put the gearbox and final drive in the sump. The Mini also featured fully independent suspension with rubber cones, developed by Issigonis's great friend Alex Moulton, and had tiny 10in wheels. The mechanical ensemble was

Two ladies, possibly on business from Porlock, seem to have lost their way. The original-style Austin-badged Mini had the wavy-line grille associated with the marque.

Supposedly the five people and the mountain of luggage shown would fit into a Mini. One has one's doubts...

The sectioned display car, caught by the camera in Dick Burzi's old styling studio behind the 'Kremlin', amply demonstrates the advantages of the transverse engine.

Basic this interior may be, but this is actually the de-luxe model of the Mini, featuring two-tone vinyl trim and carpets on the floor, in place of the cloth trim and rubber mats of the standard model.

cloaked in an uncompromising – but essentially attractive – two-box body-shell which measured little more than 10 by 4 by 4 feet.

Of course there had to be both Austin and Morris versions of the new car, so project ADO15 became the Austin Seven and the Morris Mini-Minor. In 1962 the Austin Seven was renamed Austin Mini, but otherwise the dual identity lasted until 1969, when the separate Austin and Morris badges were dropped and the car became simply the Mini. For the first few years the cars were built in either the Longbridge or the Cowley factories, but from 1968 onwards all UK Mini production was centralised at Longbridge.

In 1959 there were only saloon models, in standard or de-luxe forms, and a choice of three colours (Farina Grey, Tartan Red and Speedwell Blue for the Austins). The standard models had cloth upholstery and rubber floor mats, while de-luxe cars had two-tone vinyl trim and carpets. The Mini was always idiosyncratic in many respects, and none more so than the original cars, with their floor-mounted starter buttons, long willowy gearlevers coming out of the toe board, and sliding windows. The driving position was unusual, with the steering column

more upright and the wheel more angled than normal. The boot was derisory but the fold-down bootlid did double duty as a luggage carrier, and there was plenty of stowage space inside the car. It was never Issigonis's policy to waste space on mere mechanical components, so there was precious little room around the 848cc transverse engine.

Issigonis was arguably the greatest concept engineer ever to have designed a car, and the legacy of the Mini is now all around us. But he was never too concerned about the detail development

of his cars. Luckily the Mini suffered less from teething troubles than some later Issigonis designs. Its worst failings were the notorious tendency to leak and the weak synchromesh. Both were corrected within a year or two of production.

It took a little while for the Mini to become accepted in the marketplace, and the greatest annual production figures would only be achieved some ten or more years after its introduction. Only around 20,000 Minis were in fact made in 1959. However, BMC were quick to introduce additional models.

Right Very early Austin Seven Countryman, with the fuel filler on the 'wrong' side. It was soon also available without the wooden trim.

Below Minis coming down at the end of the assembly line at Longbridge, with A40 Farinas on the parallel track in the background.

Above The Mini van changed least over the years, retaining this simple fixed radiator grille throughout its twenty-year production period.

Left The pick-up was always one of the less common versions, with only around one pick-up being made for every ten vans.

An estate car appeared in 1960, in Austin guise called the Countryman, with a slightly longer wheelbase and overall length and at first fitted with wooden body trim. This was of course purely cosmetic and eventually the model was also offered without the wood. A van version had appeared some months before the estate but a pick-up had to wait until early 1961.

This was to be a prolific year for Mini derivatives. There were the up-market Riley and Wolseley versions, and the higher-performance Mini-Cooper (described separately). Also in 1961 the Super saloon appeared, with better equipment, additional instruments, and two-tone colour schemes à la Mini-Cooper. However, in the

following year the de-luxe and Super models were replaced by one new Super-de-luxe version. In 1964 the Minis gained Hydrolastic suspension – the interconnected hydraulic suspension system developed by Moulton and Dunlop originally for the 1100 in 1962 – and 1964 also saw the introduction of the Mini-Moke. Originally developed with an eye to military applications, the Mini-Moke was fitted with an extremely basic body which in BMC terminology was known as a 'buckboard'. Because this version was still deemed to be subject to Purchase Tax in Britain, most were sold overseas, and after 1968 the Moke was only made abroad, at first in Australia, later in Portugal.

The 1965 Motor Show saw the introduction of an automatic gearbox option, using a specially developed four-speed unit made by Automotive Products. Also in 1965 BMC had celebrated the manufacture of the millionth Mini. The original Mark I models had another two years to go before a new Mark II range was unveiled at the 1967 Motor Show. The Mark II models could be identified by their squared-up radiator grilles, bigger rear lamps and wider rear windows. The 850 models were supplemented by the Mini 1000, fitted with the 998cc engine similar to those used in the Riley, Wolseley and Cooper models. The Mini 1000 also had the Cooper-type remote gearchange. There were

Left A row of Mark II Minis with the new squared-up grille, lined up outside the sales block at Longbridge, with the 'Elephant House' (commercial vehicle showroom) in the background.

Below Mini-Moke, or masochists' delight. Rejected by the Army, it found favour in the sunnier climes of California and the Caribbean, apart from on Carnaby Street.

Left The Mark II version of the Mini Countryman featured the new 998cc engine. This is an example of the all-metal version, but you could still buy it with the wooden trim.

now 850 standard and super-de-luxe saloons, 1000 super-de-luxe saloons and estates, van, pick-up and Moke versions in the basic Austin Mini range. The final major improvement to the original Mini was the introduction of an all-synchromesh gearbox in 1968. In 1969, the second millionth Mini came off the assembly line, but at the end of the year a substantially redesigned Mini was introduced, replacing the Austin and Morris badged models.

Apart from the UK-built Minis, there were several different foreign versions. In Italy, Innocenti built Mini saloons and estate cars, as well as the Mini-Cooper. BMC in Australia built or assembled many different Minis, which were notable for having wind-down windows many years before these were fitted on the British cars. Minis would also ultimately be produced in BMC or British Leyland factories in Spain and Belgium, and were assembled from CKD kits in many more countries. A glass-fibre bodied Mini was developed for assembly in Chile.

Right from the start, the amazing road holding and handling of the Mini endeared it to road testers and the more enthusiastic driver. Even in the basic 848cc 34bhp form the Mini had excellent performance, with a 72mph

top speed like the 948cc-engined A40 Farina. Minis soon began to make their appearance in competitions, in racing as well as rallies, and although the greatest impact was made by the Mini-Cooper versions in later years, the outstanding achievement with the original 848cc version was Sir John Whitmore's triumph in the British saloon car championship in 1961.

Specifications

SEVEN/MINI MARK I 1958-67
Engine four cylinder ohv transverse, 848cc
Bore × stroke 62.9×68.3mm
Power 34bhp @ 5500rpm
Transmission four-speed manual in engine sump (automatic optional from 1965), front wheel drive
Chassis unitary construction with subframes
Wheelbase 80in (2032mm) saloon, 84.25in (2140mm) other models
Length 120.25in (3054mm) saloon, 129.9in (3299mm) other models
Width 55in (1397mm)
Height 53in (1346mm)
Weight 1380lbs (626kg)
Suspension independent with rubber cones front and rear (interconnected Hydrolastic from 1964 on saloon and Countryman models)
Brakes hydraulic
Bodywork two-door saloon, Countryman, van, pick-up

Top speed 72mph (116km/h)
Price when introduced £497 (standard saloon), £537 (de-luxe saloon), £623 (Countryman), £592 (Super Seven)
Total production (approx) 435,500 saloons, 85,500 Countrymans, 147,000 vans, 14,000 pick-ups

MINI-MOKE 1964-68
As Mini Mark I, except:
Transmission manual only
Length 120in (3048mm)
Width 51.5in (1308mm)
Height 56in (1422mm)
Weight 1176lbs (534kg)
Suspension independent with rubber cones
Bodywork open four-seater utility
Top speed 70mph (113km/h)
Price when introduced £413
Total production approx 5400

MINI MARK II 850 AND 1000 1967-69
As Mini Mark I, except:
Engine 848cc or 998cc
Bore × stroke 64.6×76.2mm (998cc)
Power 38bhp @ 5250rpm (998cc)
Width 55.5in (1410mm)
Weight 1400lbs (636kg)
Top speed 75mph (121km/h) 998cc
Price when introduced £509 (850 saloon), £579 (1000 super de-luxe saloon), £610 (1000 Countryman)
Total production (approx) 154,000 saloons, 22,500 Countrymans, 27,500 vans, 4000 pick-ups

The two-tone colour scheme and special radiator grille were identification points for the Mini-Cooper models, or as the badge correctly reads, Austin Cooper. The rapid little bolide attracted a devoted following in many European markets.

Above The Cooper interior featured two-tone upholstery, a triple-instrument pack and a remote-control gearchange.

Right The Cooper 'S' model had an extra 'S' above the bonnet badge and could be identified by its pierced wheels without wheel trims.

Mini-Cooper and Mini-Cooper 'S' 1961-1971

The enormous potential of the Mini was realised soon after its launch in 1959. BMC's Competitions Department used some of the early 848cc cars in rallying, and private entrants took the Minis into saloon car racing. The tuners and improvers – who were always amply rewarded by the BMC A-series engine – soon got busy. No-one was more keenly interested than the well-known racing car constructor from Surbiton, John Cooper.

He developed a 997cc version of the A-series engine, with twin carburettors, and fitted it in what was basically an ordinary Mini, although the modified car also benefitted from specially-developed 7in Lockheed front disc brakes and a close-ratio gearbox with remote change. George Harriman of BMC agreed to put the car into production. It was given the BMC project number of ADO50 and was introduced as the Austin and Morris Mini-Cooper models in 1961. The

model was only available in two-tone colour schemes for exterior and interior trim, looking superficially like the Super Mini introduced at the same time, but it always had its own design of radiator grille, with simple horizontal bars. It soon became a favourite trick among owners of ordinary Minis to paint their cars' roofs white or black, imitating the Coopers.

By dint of stretching the bore of the Mini engine to 70.6mm, a 1071cc engine was developed. This necessitated re-jigging the block, changing the bore centres, and it was one of few A-series that were actually oversquare. The bigger engine gave 70bhp and had a nitrided crankshaft. It was fitted in the Mini-Cooper 'S' of 1963, which also had servo-assisted brakes and ventilated wheels. Wider 4.5in rims and an extra fuel tank were usually specified, while alternative final drive ratios, a sump guard and an oil cooler were available as options.

In 1964 two alternative versions of the 'S' were brought out. The even more oversquare 970cc model (of which barely 1,000 were made) was a

bit of a 'homologation special' built with an eye to saloon car racing. More important was the long-stroke 1275cc model, which after a few months replaced the 1071cc car altogether. Also in 1964 the ordinary Mini-Cooper was fitted with a 998cc engine instead of the 997cc version, seemingly a small change but bringing the car's engine into line with the Riley Elf and Wolseley Hornet models, and late in the year the Mini-Cooper models were modified with the adoption of Hydrolastic suspension.

Mini-Cooper Mark II models followed in October 1967, their bodies being modified in tandem with the ordinary Minis, now incorporating wider rear windows, bigger rear light units and slightly modified radiator grilles. At the end of 1969 the 998cc model was discontinued, but a Mini-Cooper 'S' Mark III was introduced as part of the new Mini ADO20 range, with internal door hinges and wind-down windows. Only 1500 or so cars of this type were made at Longbridge (apart from overseas production) before the Mini-Cooper disappeared in mid-1971,

Had he not been disqualified because of a technical infringement, Rauno Aaltonen would have been second in the 1966 Monte Carlo rally, despite the somewhat crumpled state of the front wing of his Austin Mini-Cooper.

Below All Coopers had twin carburettors but only the 'S' model featured the brake servo seen here.

Below New badges and a new grille were introduced on the Mark II models launched at the 1967 Motor Show.

victim of the Stokes-inspired programme to reduce the model range (and to avoid paying royalties to John Cooper!).

In overseas markets, Mini-Coopers and 'S' models had long been produced in Australia, with partial CKD kits being sent out from England. The Italian BMC licensees, later a British Leyland subsidiary, Innocenti, also produced the Mini-Cooper as well as ordinary Mini Saloons and estates. This was somewhat better specified than the English versions, having for instance a rev. counter as standard. There were also Spanish Mini-Coopers made by AUTHI in a factory that would later turn out Opel Corsas and Vauxhall Novas for General Motors.

The Mini-Cooper was quickly put to good use by BMC's Competitions Department and the company was rewarded with a string of victories, beginning with Pat Moss's win in the 1962 Tulip Rally. The Mini-Cooper 'S' would prove an even more formidable weapon, scoring most famously the three wins in the Monte Carlo Rally in 1964, 1965 and 1967, apart from adding

numerous other laurels to BMC's crown. Possibly because the Abingdon-based Competitions Department displayed a bias in favour of the Morris-badged models, most of the famous victories were won by Morris Mini-Coopers – but major rally wins in Austin Mini-Coopers included those of Timo Makinen in the 1965 1000 Lakes rally, Paddy Hopkirk in the 1965 Circuit of Ireland (repeated in 1967), Rauno Aaltonen in the 1965 RAC Rally, and Hopkirk in the 1967 Acropolis Rally. Regardless of the badging of individual cars, any Mini-Cooper victory was the cause for legitimate rejoicing throughout BMC and indeed throughout the nation.

BMC was not involved in saloon car racing, leaving this to private entrants, of whom John Love won the 1962 British Saloon Car Championship. John Cooper had a team of Mini-Cooper saloon racers, from time to time numbering John Rhodes, John Handley and Warwick Banks among his drivers. Banks was 1964 European saloon car champion, and Rhodes won this title in 1968. The Tyrrell and

Broadspeed teams also campaigned Mini-Coopers in saloon racing. In 1967 a BMC-entered Mini-Cooper 'S' won its class in the 3 hour race at Sebring, and private entrants had numerous successes in Australia, New Zealand and Europe. Works cars were run in the 1969 Rallycross championship, where John Rhodes was second overall in a fuel-injected Mini-Cooper 'S'.

Above The 'S' version of the Mark II also got a new badge.

The Liverpool constabulary were enthusiastic users of Mini-Coopers, and here they show off the latest Mark II 'S' models in 1968.

Above The rear end of a Mark II 'S' model shows the bigger rear light units and the wider rear window, improvements common to all Minis at this time.

Specifications

MINI-COOPER MARK I 1961-67
Engine four cylinder ohv transverse, 997cc (998cc from 1964)
Bore × stroke 62.4×81.3mm (997cc), 64.6×76.2mm (998cc)
Power 55bhp @ 6000rpm (997cc), 55bhp @ 5800rpm (998cc)
Transmission four-speed manual in engine sump, front wheel drive
Chassis unitary construction with subframes
Wheelbase 80in (2032mm)
Length 120.25in (3054mm)
Width 55in (1397mm)
Height 53in (1346mm)
Weight 1400lbs (636kg)
Suspension independent with rubber cones front and rear (interconnected Hydrolastic from 1964)
Brakes hydraulic, discs at front
Bodywork two-door saloon
Top speed 85mph (137km/h)
Price when introduced £679
Total production approx 12,600 (997cc), 18,000 (998cc)

MINI-COOPER 'S' 1071cc 1963-64
As Mini-Cooper Mark I, except:
Engine 1071cc
Bore × stroke 70.6×68.3mm
Power 70bhp @ 6000rpm
Weight 1410lbs (640kg)
Top speed 95mph (153km/h)
Price when introduced £695
Total production approx 2100

MINI-COOPER 'S' 970cc 1964
As 1071cc model, except:
Engine 970cc
Bore × stroke 70.6×61.9mm
Power 65bhp @ 6500rpm
Price when introduced £693
Total production approx 500

MINI-COOPER 'S' 1275cc 1964-67
As 1071cc model, except:
Engine 1275cc
Bore × stroke 70.6×81.3mm
Power 76bhp @ 5800rpm
Top speed 97mph (156km/h)
Price when introduced £778
Total production approx 6400

MINI-COOPER MARK II 1967-69
As Mini-Cooper Mark I 998cc, except:
Top speed 90mph (145km/h)
Price when introduced £631
Total production approx 9900

MINI-COOPER 'S' MARK II 1967-69
As Mini-Cooper 'S' 1275cc, except:
Price when introduced £849
Total production approx 2400

MINI-COOPER 'S' MARK III 1970-71
As Mini-Cooper 'S' Mark II, except:
Weight 1525lbs (692kg)
Suspension last few cars may have had rubber cones rather than Hydrolastic
Price when introduced £942
Total production estimated 1500 (plus possibly 18,000 CKD units for assembly abroad)

Above The Austin 1100 made its appearance a good year later than the Morris model, with typical grille and badge differences.

The 1100 facia was hardly worthy of the name, a narrow strip with only the bare essentials. The unmarked 'flick' switches could be confusing, and any extra controls had to be situated on add-on panels below the main facia.

Above Rivalling the much bigger Cambridge for interior roominess, the 1100 in Austin guise favoured pastel colours for the trim, adding to the overall impression of airy spaciousness.

1100 and 1300 1963-1974

The second Issigonis-designed BMC front wheel drive car, project ADO16, arrived in Morris form in August 1962, but Austin dealers had to wait just over a year before the equivalent Austin 1100 appeared in their showrooms. The 1100 did not have the same sort of impact as the Mini and tends now to be either maligned or forgotten, but in its day it was the finest small family saloon available anywhere in the world. It was the best-selling car in Britain for a number of years, and BMC turned out more than 2.1 million units under six different badges. Derivatives were made in Australia, South Africa, Italy and Spain. The Mini and the 1100 were tremendously successful in many export markets, and made Austin and Morris household names in some quite surprising places. The contemporary commentator who described the new model as a 'world car' must have been blessed with the gift of second sight.

The transverse engine, gearbox in sump and front wheel drive power package closely followed the lines established by the Mini. The faithful A-series engine was bored out to 1098cc and gave approximately 48bhp. The 1100 was the first car to feature the interconnected Hydrolastic suspension system – ill-advised early advertising claimed that the 1100 "floated on fluid" – which at that time gave greater comfort, with better road holding and handling, than any conventionally suspended car could offer. The front disc brakes were still somewhat of a novelty, especially on a car in this class, and the 1100 was one of the first cars to offer a 'sealed' cooling system.

The usual expert Issigonis packaging had produced a car little longer than the A40 Farina but with an extra 6 inches in the wheelbase offering virtually the same amount of room inside as an A60 Cambridge. The boot was admittedly smallish, low down, and awkward to load with its shallow upwards-opening lid. There was unusually happy co-operation between Issigonis and BMC's styling consultant, Pininfarina – unusual because Issigonis would often proclaim his contempt for all stylists (except Pininfarina) and because such an attractive and well-proportioned little car was produced despite what must have been one of the most tightly packaged layouts in the history of car design. The interior style was perhaps disappointing, being in accordance with Issigonis's minimalist ideas – a narrow ribbon doing duty as 'facia', with a rectangular instrument pack incorporating a strip-type speedometer.

Only a four-door saloon was originally offered, in standard or de-luxe versions. Automatic transmission, using the AP gearbox found on the Mini, became available in 1965, and a two-door Countryman estate car joined the range in 1966. This had a more vertical rear end with a large top-hinged tailgate, and a folding rear seat. BMC stopped short of offering an 1100 hatchback as such, although some conversions were offered by outside companies. The first 1100 two-door saloons also appeared in 1966 but for the first two years were sold exclusively in certain export markets.

For the 1967 Motor Show the range received a facelift, with the tailfins cut back and new radiator grilles. There were now two models, a 1275cc-engined Austin 1300 appearing for the first time. De-luxe and super-de-luxe versions had different grilles and facias; the super-de-luxe continued the original theme but the 1100 Mark II de-luxe had a round speedometer sitting in a central box on the parcels shelf, Mini-style. Two-door models became available on the home market for the first time. An export-only model was the Austin America, a two-door 1300 with automatic transmission and a de-

Above A later generation would describe the 1100 Countryman as a three-door hatchback, but the term had yet to be invented in 1966.

Above The America interior, with headrests, rocker switches and a steering column lock. The model was only available with automatic transmission.

toxed engine to meet new US regulations. It held no great appeal for North American customers and only lasted two or three seasons. Some later examples were sold in Switzerland.

Even with the bigger engine the Austin 1300 was beginning to appear under-powered in comparison with its main rival, the Ford Cortina. An attempt to redress the balance came with the 1969 introduction of the Austin 1300GT, which had a 70bhp engine tuned to MG or Riley 1300 specification with twin carburettors. It was only offered in four-door form. A vinyl roof, fancy wheeltrims, an MG/Riley style facia with three dials including a rev. counter, and some strident colours completed the transformation. Performance was usefully improved, with a 93mph top speed, and the GT model earned its own small-scale following.

The final Mark III models came in 1971, in 1100 and 1300 two- and four-door versions and a 1300 Countryman. It was purely a cosmetic exercise but the Mark IIIs did gain a much neater wooden facia with round instruments. There were also face-level ventilation vents for the first time. The range soldiered on into 1974, continuing in limited production even after the Allegro replacement had been

Above Another effort at selling a small saloon car in the USA. The 1968 America was suitably modified to meet the new emissions and safety regulations.

Right Mark II 1100s coming off the assembly lines. The new full-width grille was not really a stylistic improvement.

launched. Small numbers of saloons were still made for export in 1975.

Of foreign versions of the 1100/1300 design, the South African built Apache and the Spanish built Victoria were both badged Austin. They shared a Michelotti restyled body with a new front end (very Triumph-like) and a built-out boot added onto the original centre section. Innocenti in Italy produced the IM3 and J4 variations. In Australia, BMC ended up making the

unique five-door Morris Nomad, based on the 1300 shell but with the Maxi ohc 1.5-litre engine and five speed gearbox.

For all its undoubted technical brilliance, the 1100/1300 was always a car curiously devoid of character, in total contrast to the Mini. But perhaps this was the secret behind its universal acceptability. In old age, its reputation has been dramatically sullied by its well-known propensity for terminal corrosion.

A Mark II model shows off its cropped tailfins.

The interior of the basic Mark II 1100 was completely re-vamped, its not very attractive door casings and this Mini-inspired central instrument box looking a bit home-made.

Specifications

1100 MARK I 1963-67
Engine four cylinder ohv transverse, 1098cc
Bore × stroke 64.6×83.7mm
Power 48bhp @ 5100rpm
Transmission four-speed manual in engine sump (automatic optional from 1965), front wheel drive
Chassis unitary construction with subframes
Wheelbase 93.5in (2375mm)
Length 146.75in (3727mm)
Width 60.4in (1534mm)
Height 52.75in (1340mm)
Weight 1800lbs (817kg)
Suspension independent with interconnected Hydrolastic
Brakes hydraulic, discs at front
Bodywork four-door saloon, two-door saloon (export only), Countryman
Top speed 78mph (126km/h)
Price when introduced £593 (four-door saloon), £712 (Countryman)
Total production approx 373,000 saloons, 15,800 Countrymans

1100 MARK II and 1300 1967-71
As 1100 Mark I, except:
Engine 1098cc or 1275cc
Bore × stroke 70.6×81.3mm (1275cc)
Power 58bhp @ 5250rpm (1275cc)
Top speed 88mph (142km/h) (1275cc)
Price when introduced 1100 saloons £647-£696, 1300 saloons £672-£720, 1300 Countryman £770
Total production approx 147,500 (1100 saloons), 229,500 (1300 saloons), 1000 (1100 Countrymans), 20,000 (1300 Countrymans)

AMERICA 1968-71
As 1300, except:
Engine 1275cc
Power 60bhp @ 5250rpm
Transmission automatic only
Bodywork two-door saloon only
Price not available in home market
Total production approx 59,500

1100 AND 1300 MARK III 1971-74
As 1100 Mark II and 1300, except:
Price when introduced 1100 saloons £806-£877, 1300 saloons £872-£903, 1300 Countryman £977
Total production approx 63,500 (1100 saloons), 138,000 (1300 saloons), 20,000 (1300 Countrymans)

1300GT 1969-74
As 1300, except:
Power 70bhp @ 6000rpm
Transmission manual only
Weight 1900lbs (863kg)
Bodywork four-door saloon only
Top speed 93mph (150km/h)
Price when introduced £910
Total production approx 52,000

Although an 1100 Mark II Countryman was available, most models with this body style now had the 1300 engine and therefore this version of the grille, seen also on the America. A bit of symbolic wood trim was added to the flanks.

Right The Mark III range with simplified grilles was launched in 1971. One strip denotes 1100, three strips 1300!

Above The 1300 GT interior was unrelieved black vinyl, with a triple instrument layout first seen on the Riley Kestrel and incorporating a rev. counter.

Right The 1300 GT had this unique grille, a vinyl roof and fancy wheeltrims, but was only available with four doors.

Among 1100 models, only the Vanden Plas Princess version was offered with a sunroof, all the better to accommodate contemporary hairdos. This is probably the original 1963 prototype or Motor Show car, as the mock-up numberplate 'DEV 1' (for Development car no 1) was often seen on Vanden Plas experimental cars.

Vanden Plas Princess 1100 and 1300 1964-1974

Someone once said that as a make of car Vanden Plas was as artificial a creation as de Soto – by which the commentator meant to be kind to neither make. But Vanden Plas did trade on its impeccable reputation as a coachbuilder, which persisted long after coachbuilding techniques had been consigned to the history books, and after Vanden Plas cars had become products of the assembly lines at Longbridge or Cowley with only their final luxury trim fitted in the old Vanden Plas factory. There is no doubt that the essential Englishness of Vanden Plas furnishings held a great degree of appeal for many car buyers in the 1960s, not least to women, at whom the 1100 model was unashamedly aimed under the slogan "To-day's smart car is a Vanden Plas". These same qualities have now made the Princess 1100/1300 such a popular car among Japanese enthusiasts.

The Vanden Plas version of the 1100 was launched at the 1963 Motor Show, and apart from the miniature version of the Vanden Plas radiator grille and the usual wood-and-leather interior, there was no real difference between

Proof that those picnic tables were not only for show. Proof also of the roominess of the 1100, even if the front seats are well forward in this picture.

this car and the MG 1100 whose twin-carburettor engine the Vanden Plas inherited. Furthermore, although this was not a point which BMC cared to make public, the first three years' production was entirely built and trimmed at Longbridge and never got anywhere near the Vanden Plas factory. Later models did however make the detour to Kingsbury, by which time production of the basic car had been switched from Longbridge to Cowley. An optional extra unique to the Vanden Plas model was a sunroof,

which involved taking each car to be so equipped off the production line and farming it out to the nearest branch of Weathershields.

In the USA, BMC had been selling small numbers of the Vanden Plas Princess 3 litre, and it was thought that there might also be a market for the smaller model. The MG 1100 was at this time doing respectably well in North America, where a two-door version known as the 'Sportsedan' was marketed. To latch on to MG's traditionally strong image in the USA,

Below The typical Vanden Plas recessed instruments were supplemented by this switch panel, in flagrant imitation of Rolls-Royce practice, but the steering wheel and bent-wire indicator stalk betray the car's humble origins.

Right One could not complain about the standard of the interior appointments on the Vanden Plas version of the 1100.

The front was unchanged on the later 1300 model, cropped tailfins indicating that this is a Mark II.

BMC decided to market the small Vanden Plas as the 'MG Princess' in the States, although this experiment stopped after only 150 or so cars had been shipped out. Apart from the additional MG badges on the radiator grille, hub caps, etc., they did not in any way differ from the standard article.

In the spring of 1967 the small Princess became available with the 1275cc engine as an option, at the same time as this was offered in the MG, Riley and Wolseley versions of the design but a good six months before the bigger engine was offered to Austin or Morris customers. These early cars were only ever in very limited production as BMC did not yet have the capacity to make the 1275cc engines on any large scale. At the 1967 Motor Show the Vanden Plas models became the 1100 Mark II and the 1300, sharing the modified tailfins and new tail lights of the other 1100/1300 models. The 1300 had a single-carburettor engine and was offered with the option of an automatic gearbox. The 1100 Mark II was discontinued a few months later, leaving the 1300 to carry on alone.

In late 1968 it became the 1300 Mark II, with manual gearbox models receiving a more powerful twin-carburettor engine, while the automatic versions stuck to the original single-carburettor unit. There was very little in the way of further change to the model. It continued to sell well, if not spectacularly, to a traditionally-minded clientele, to women buyers, and to well-off retired middle class customers. One imagines Eastbourne being full of them. It was one of the longest-lived versions of the original ADO 16 design, surviving well into 1974, until finally replaced by the much less attractive Allegro-based Vanden Plas 1500.

Specifications

VANDEN PLAS PRINCESS 1100 1963-67
Engine four cylinder ohv transverse, 1098cc (1275cc optional in 1967)
Bore × stroke 64.6×83.7mm
Power 55bhp @ 5500rpm
Transmission four-speed manual in engine sump, front wheel drive
Chassis unitary construction with subframes
Wheelbase 93.5in (2375mm)
Length 146.75in (3727mm)
Width 60.4in (1534mm)
Height 52.75in (1340mm)
Weight 1950lbs (885kg)
Suspension independent with interconnected Hydrolastic

Brakes hydraulic, discs at front
Bodywork four-door saloon
Top speed 85mph (137km/h)
Price when introduced £896
Total production 16,007 (including 1100 Mk II and also including 154 'MG Princess' cars for the USA in 1964-66)

VANDEN PLAS PRINCESS 1100 MARK II
1967-68
As 1100, except:
Price when introduced £975

VANDEN PLAS PRINCESS 1300 1967-68
As 1100, except:
Engine 1275cc
Bore × stroke 70.6×81.3mm
Power 58bhp @ 5250rpm
Transmission automatic optional
Top speed 88mph (142km/h)
Price when introduced £1000
Total production 23,734 (including 1967 Mark I cars with 1275cc engines, and 1300 Mark II)

VANDEN PLAS PRINCESS 1300 MARK II
1968-74
As 1300, except:
Power 65bhp @ 5750rpm (manual gearbox), 60bhp @ 5250rpm (automatic)
Top speed 90mph (145km/h)
Price when introduced £1087
Total production see 1300 model

Below Typical of Issigonis's philosophy, the facia was what you would expect after the 1100. This was the first BMC car to have a separate fresh-air ventilation system, with adjustable air vents at either end of the parcels shelf.

Left With the 1800, Issigonis tried to redefine the concept of the large family car. Almost universally admired by contemporary observers, it failed to sell in the hoped-for numbers.

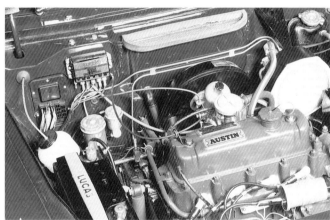

1800 and 2200 1964-1975

ADO 17, launched as the Austin 1800 in 1964, was confidently expected by its backers to become Issigonis's and BMC's hat-trick, the third successful front wheel drive car to complete the line-up started with the Mini and the 1100. Instead it was a case of third time unlucky. There was nothing wrong with the concept of the 1800, and once it had got over its only too well-publicised teething troubles it emerged as one of the best family saloons of the decade. Launched into that ebullient decade when British automotive engineers led the world, the 1800 was chosen as Car of the Year. While this may be considered at best a dubious acclaim, it does prove that the car made a big impact throughout Europe and was admired by hard-bitten motoring hacks.

The problem was that the 1800 fell between every possible stool. Intended as a Cambridge replacement, it ended up being too big and too expensive. Intended to be powerful, it was so heavy that performance was only adequate, and it was no match for nimbler lightweights such as Ford's Cortina or Vauxhall's Victor. Intended to be stylish, Pininfarina's original proposals were sadly compromised by

Issigonis, who even felt smug about his 'improvements'. The 1800 was not a competitor for the new performance-orientated lightweight saloons offered by Ford and Vauxhall, nor was it stylish, powerful or exclusive enough to cut any ice in the growing executive car sector, typified by the Rover and Triumph 2000 models. BMC expected the car to sell in vast numbers, but it never lived up to expectations. The 1800 was the first visible – and very ominous – crack in BMC's as yet otherwise unruffled corporate facade.

Yet the 1800 had many qualities. It was the roomiest family saloon on the market, and, unusually for an Issigonis-designed car, even had a decently-sized boot, but was still less than 14ft long. It was a supremely comfortable car to ride in, Hydrolastic being better than conventional suspension systems of the time. The roadholding and handling were excellent and inspired a great deal of confidence. It was an extremely strong car, with an unusually high figure for torsional stiffness, and BMC confidently stated that it was in effect a long-life car. On the other side of the coin, the driving position was typically awful, the steering was heavy – no power assistance before late 1967 – and the cable-operated gearchange and lack of

The under-bonnet view of the 1800, with radiator expansion tank, brake servo, and the infamous shock absorber to stop engine rock.

synchromesh on first conspired to produce a monumentally dreadful result. The interior and facia were as spartan as on any Issigonis car, even if you could stow an umbrella on the full-width parcels shelf under the ribbon type facia. Worst of all, the early cars suffered from all sorts of problems due to rushed development and patchy build quality, including the infamous wrongly calibrated dipstick. Another peculiarity, a last-minute amendment, was the miniature shock absorber attached to the engine mount to tame engine vibrations. It worked and was immediately hailed as yet another BMC technical breakthrough.

Inevitably the Austin was followed by Morris and Wolseley derivatives. There were no alternative body styles in the UK, but BMC in Australia offered a pick-up and in 1970 brought out the Austin X6 Kimberley and Tasman models, with six cylinder E-series ohc engines of 2.2 litres, as well as much modified body shells. At home, some improvements to the basic interior design were made, including a centre console on the parcels shelf introduced

In 1968 the 1800 went into Mark II form. The up-dated radiator grille was similar to that of the new 1300, and there were little fins at the back.

Right Later 1800s featured a centre console breaking up the wide open space of the parcels shelf. This is actually a Mark III, with the handbrake between the seats.

in early 1967, and power steering became optional in 1967. A Mark II version appeared in 1968, with a revised radiator grille, little add-on tailfins, wheels increased in size from 13in to 14in, and an automatic gearbox option which featured primary drive from engine to gearbox by chain and a facia-mounted gear selector. Then there was the 1800 'S' model, with a twin-carburettor engine tuned to almost MGB specification and 100mph performance. This was in many ways quite the best of the range but it only lasted until 1972, when Mark III models were introduced. Yet another radiator grille design was accompanied by further improvements to the interior trim, and the under-facia pistol grip handbrake was replaced by a conventional lever between the seats.

The basic single-carburettor 1800 continued in Mark III form and the 'S' model was replaced by the 2200, which followed the lead given by BMC Australia by adopting this development of the ohc E-series engine found in the Austin Maxi. It gave the ageing car a useful performance boost, with a 104mph top speed as well as much greater refinement. Alas, camshaft breakages were not unknown on early cars. On the 2200 there was a 'proper' facia, wood-trimmed and with round

instruments. There were Morris and Wolseley versions, as ever, and it is interesting that the Wolseley Six sold more than the Austin and Morris 2200 models together. The last versions of the 1800 and 2200 'land crab' were discontinued in 1975 to make way for the new 18-22 range, soon renamed Princess.

The strength and ruggedness of the 1800's basic design was amply demonstrated by the appearance of large numbers in the more strenuous rallies of the late 1960s, including the London-Sydney Marathon in December 1968 when Paddy Hopkirk, with co-drivers Nash and Poole, finished

second overall. In the 1970 World Cup Rally from London to Mexico BL's works team concentrated on the Maxi and the Triumph 2.5 PI, but Abingdon prepared five 1800s for private entrants, and two 1800s finished respectably high up in the result list, coming 9th and 11th overall.

The 1800 was the sort of car which you had to take trouble with, but once you got to know it the rewards were great. In this respect and in many of its idiosyncracies it invites comparison with the Citroën DS19. This comment, at least, should placate the spirit of the late Sir Alec Issigonis.

The 1800 Mark III of 1972 was supplemented by the 2200 model. The grille was slightly different, and the car had by now lost its overriders.

Below A late-model 1800 Mark III, almost in the last year of production, shows off the little tail fins which were added in 1968.

Below The 2200 engine was a remarkable engineering feat, the only example of an in-line six-cylinder engine installed transversely in a front-wheel drive car. It needed to be compact!

Specifications

1800 MARK I 1964-68
Engine four cylinder ohv transverse, 1798cc
Bore × stroke 80.3×88.9mm
Power 80bhp @ 5000rpm
Transmission four-speed manual in engine sump, front wheel drive
Chassis unitary construction
Wheelbase 106in (2692mm)
Length 164.25in (4172mm)
Width 67in (1702mm)
Height 55.5in (1410mm)
Weight 2645lbs (1200kg)
Suspension independent with interconnected Hydrolastic
Brakes hydraulic, discs at front
Bodywork four-door saloon
Top speed 90mph (145km/h)
Price when introduced £769 (standard model), £809 (de-luxe model)
Total production approx 110,000

1800 MARK II 1968-72
As 1800 Mark I, except:
Power 86bhp @ 5300rpm
Transmission automatic optional
Length 166.2in (4221mm)
Top speed 93mph (150km/h)
Price when introduced £1021
Total production approx 74,000 (including 'S' models)

1800 'S' 1969-72
As 1800 Mark II, except:
Power 96bhp @ 5700rpm
Transmission manual only
Top speed 99mph (159km/h)
Price when introduced £1139
Total production see 1800 Mark II

1800 MARK III 1972-75
As 1800 Mark II, except:
Price when introduced £1246
Total production approx 26,000

2200 1972-75
As 1800 Mark III, except:
Engine six cylinder ohc transverse, 2227cc
Bore × stroke 76.2×81.3mm
Power 110bhp @ 5250rpm
Length 166.75in (4235mm)
Weight 2620lbs (1189kg)
Top speed 104mph (167km/h)
Price when introduced £1371
Total production 20,865 (Austin and Morris together)

As originally seen at the 1967 Motor Show the Austin 3 litre had these square headlamps, which gave the car a vaguely Chinese look.

Below The entire centre section was borrowed from the 1800 so the 3 litre's looks were inevitably predictable.

3 litre 1967-1971

From 1958 to 1964 Austin and BMC had pushed forward with incredible momentum, launching new model after new model, producing more interesting and better cars, most of them successful, some of them all-time greats. Leonard Lord had by now stepped down from the day-to-day running of the corporation, becoming BMC's president and effectively leaving George Harriman in charge. Alec Issigonis became BMC's technical director. That was perhaps a mistake. Great designer though he was, Issigonis had little time for administrative work and no time at all for committees or board meetings. The launch of the 1800 in 1964 marked the end of an era for BMC, although this was not realised at the time. Behind the scenes, there were already efforts to find a partner to merge with. The financial results were slowly worsening although a dramatic drop in profits would not emerge until 1967. Output was slowly declining after a high reached in the 1963-64 season. The model programme was getting out of hand, with too many different cars overlapping in the marketplace and fighting for space on the Longbridge and Cowley assembly lines.

During this period, BMC and Jaguar merged in the summer of 1966. BMC also merged with the Pressed Steel Company, the important Cowley-based body manufacturer. The merger with Jaguar brought a dowry in the form of an enviable range of prestige saloons, and should have been an opportunity for BMC to give up its elderly six-cylinder range, but the corporation was firmly committed to a replacement model for the Westminster, and had in fact 'frozen' the ADO61 design some years previously. That it was not introduced until 1967 – and then only tentatively – was a reflection on the company's cashflow position.

The idea of producing a bigger and better 1800 was in a way quite logical. One also suspects that it was one way to get value for money out of some quite expensive but under-utilised tooling. It imposed unfortunate restrictions on the styling of the new big saloon car, and also gave it exactly the same interior package as the smaller, less prestigious model. Even BMC fought shy of producing a 3-litre front wheel drive saloon so the car was given an in-line engine and rear wheel drive. Not content with using the existing C-series, an almost brand-new engine with a seven main bearing crankshaft was developed, allegedly based on BMC Australia's 2.4-litre 'Blue Streak' design, but with the same dimensions and 2912cc capacity as the outgoing

Above The interior of the de-luxe model was quite civilized, but trim was Ambla rather than leather, the car still had that strip speedometer and the angle of the steering column was more bus-like than strictly necessary.

Above Production 3 litres were fitted with double round headlamps, and quarterlights were added to the front doors.

Left The longer rear end actually came off quite well. This was perhaps the most attractive view of the car.

Westminster engine. Apart from the Austin 3 litre, the only BMC model to use the new engine was the MGC.

To accommodate the six a new front end was grafted on to the 1800 bodyshell, and for good measure a new rear end to balance the proportions of the car. The suspension was all independent and was based on the Hydrolastic system but with the added refinement of self-levelling at the rear. Unfortunately this was driven by the engine and was set to maintain the level of the car such as it was whenever the engine was started. If you loaded the boot before starting the engine, your 3 litre would determinedly drag its tail all day long. The interior was on the basic side, with Ambla-upholstered 1800 type seats, the usual BMC strip speedometer, and an oddly cranked gear lever.

The model made its bow at the 1967 Motor Show, originally fitted with rectangular headlamps. It was expressly stated that the new car would at first be built in small numbers, which would be passed out to favoured customers for assessment so that modifications based on their suggestions could be incorporated in the final design. Surprisingly enough the early owners were so pleased with the car that the only revisions introduced were twin round headlamps, a higher final drive and the addition of quarterlights in the front doors. More important was the emergence after the first full year's production of the 3 litre de-luxe with more sound-proofing and better seats.

The car was comfortable and by now comparatively luxurious. Power steering was standard, with overdrive or an automatic gearbox being optional. But it offered no more room than an 1800 and acceleration was slower than an 1800 'S'. Brochures told us "comfort is a 3 litre word" and tried to promote a chauffeur-driven, Whitehallish image. But the car lacked the prestige or appeal of a Rover 3½ litre, a Triumph 2.5 PI or any of the Jaguars. It was the wrong car at the wrong time; the late 1960s saw Ford and Vauxhall also finding it difficult to maintain sales of their big six-cylinder models, while Humber had given up the struggle.

There were proposals for both Vanden Plas and Wolseley versions of the 3 litre, and it is possible that the car might have done rather better if it had carried a more prestigious name and radiator grille. One car was apparently fitted with the Rover 3½-litre V8 engine, which certainly transformed the performance, but the idea was promptly vetoed by Rover as well as Jaguar; Solihull's excuse was the lack of V8 production capacity, but they would obviously not welcome an in-house competitor for their own products.

For three years the 3 litre production line in the Cowley factory remained a singularly quiet and peaceful spot in an otherwise bustling factory. But in early 1971, when the decks were being cleared of unwanted baggage in preparation for Marina production, the 3 litre was inevitably a casualty.

Specifications

3 LITRE 1967-71
Engine six cylinder ohv, 2912cc
Bore × stroke 83.3×88.9mm
Power 124bhp @ 4500rpm
Transmission four-speed manual (overdrive or automatic optional)
Chassis unitary construction
Wheelbase 115.5in (2934mm)
Length 185.75in (4718mm)
Width 66.75in (1695mm)
Height 56.75in (1441mm)
Weight 3290lbs (1494kg)
Suspension independent with interconnected Hydrolastic, self-levelling at rear
Brakes hydraulic, discs at front
Bodywork four-door saloon
Top speed 100mph (161km/h)
Price when introduced £1418
Total production 9992

First thoughts for the Maxi in 1966. A stunted 1800 with a rear hatch and an over-fussy grille was unlikely to please many faithful Cambridge customers.

The 1969 Maxi as launched. The revised front end was simpler and more harmonious but rather bland. Not much could be done about the rest of the car.

Maxi 1969-1981

The Maxi was the last complete car designed by the Issigonis team. Once it became clear that the 1800 was too big and expensive to provide the desired Austin Cambridge replacement, work was begun on a smaller car which would be fitted with a 1½-litre engine and which could hopefully be sold at a cheaper price. Following the example of the Renault 16, introduced in 1965, it was decided to make the new car a hatchback. Issigonis as always insisted on the maximum interior package, and to save money it was decided to use those expensively-tooled 1800 doors on the new car. The early prototypes photographed in 1966 looked decidedly strange.

Finally, BMC embarked on a new engine design, virtually the corporation's first all-new engine since 1954. It was laid out with a single overhead camshaft and started out as a 1.3-litre unit, with the possibility of enlarging to 1.5 litres, but the use of siamesed bores meant that it would be difficult to increase the size beyond that limit. It was always expected that larger versions of the E-series would have six cylinders. A distinct novelty for the 1960s was the choice of a five-speed gearbox with an overdrive top. It had synchromesh on all forward ratios but inherited the unfortunate cable change from the 1800.

When BMC and Leyland merged in 1968 the new car was getting ready to be launched, but when Leyland boss Donald Stokes saw the prototype he immediately gave orders to improve the styling as much as was possible, without adding drastically to the tooling budget. A new front end was developed, while the interior, notably the facia, was also re-designed. These alterations delayed the introduction of the new model for a year, during which all sorts of rumours concerning the new BMC 1500 circulated in the press. When the Austin Maxi finally arrived in the spring of 1969 it did not live up to expectations.

It was admired for its spaciousness, its comfort and above all for its clever versatility, with the hatchback and a rear seat which could fold either way and which in combination with reclining front seats enabled the creation of a makeshift double bed. The road holding and handling were well up to the standards usual for BMC front wheel drive Hydrolastic cars. But the Maxi was considered ugly, even in comparison with the 1800, the interior was still basic and the ergonomics far from perfect, the 1500 engine was not sufficiently powerful for the car and the gearchange was memorably awful.

BMC's hopes for the Maxi were wildly optimistic, with thoughts of 250,000 or more cars per year. Unsold cars soon began to stockpile in hastily-rented depots in the South Midlands. One former hangar used for this

The second-generation Maxi in 1750 HL form. This model originally had the twin-carburettor engine which later became the preserve of the HLS model.

purpose held a wide variety of birdlife, whose natural products caused a lot of damage to the paintwork on the new Maxis. A senior British Leyland manager who must have remembered the Duke of Wellington's advice to Queen Victoria in the matter of sparrows in the Crystal Palace ("Try sparrowhawks, Ma'am") seriously suggested buying a number of cats. Instead, production in the brand new E-series engine factory at Cofton Hackett near Longbridge and on the Maxi assembly line at Cowley was hastily reduced, and the engineers got busy trying to make the Maxi acceptable to the public.

A much-improved car was launched at the 1970 Motor Show. By juggling the crankshaft about, the stroke had been lengthened and capacity increased to 1748cc (the original 1485cc version stayed in production). There was a rod-operated gearchange, the interior was brightened up with a wood facia (although the facia always retained the look of a Ford Cortina Mark II reject), and a new radiator grille and badge gave the front end a slightly less bland look. Two years later, the 1750 HL model offered a twin-carburettor engine.

By then British Leyland had come to accept the inevitable: the Maxi was never going to be the best-selling

The Maxi engine bay was still on the tight side. The big shield in front of the engine was needed to keep the distributor dry, often a problem on the original transverse-engined Austin cars.

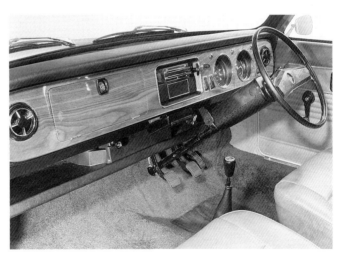

The 1970 improvements to the interior consisted chiefly of this wood capping over the facia.

Cambridge replacement that had been intended. Throughout the 1970s the best-selling mid-range Leyland saloon was the Morris Marina. The Maxi did eventually establish its own niche in the marketplace, although with home market sales averaging 30,000 cars per year it was quite a small one. It must

be remembered that before the advent of the Chrysler Alpine in 1976 no other British manufacturer offered a comparable five-door family saloon car, but there is little doubt that the discouraging reception given to the Maxi did bias British Leyland against the idea of hatchback cars, in

"... and a cuddly toy." This somehow rather suggestive picture was intended to demonstrate Maxi versatility. Rather nicer was the original 1969 advertisement which showed an elderly couple camping in a Maxi, complete with Teasmade.

The Maxi 2 was the final facelift for the ageing model, with new wheeltrims and bumpers, and the new corporate Austin Morris blue wing badge on the radiator grille.

consequence of which their next two front wheel drive models, the Allegro and the Princess, emerged as conventional four-door saloons.

In the early days some thought was given to a notchback four-door version of the Maxi, and this would very likely have been marketed under the Morris name. It looked even uglier than the five-door model and was hastily abandoned after the BMC-Leyland merger. Instead the Morris Oxford stayed in production until 1971 when the Morris Marina was introduced. It then became the accepted Leyland policy to market the advanced front wheel drive cars under the Austin banner, with the Morris name being used for conventional rear wheel drive cars, but this policy was always somewhat flexible and some cars such as the Mini ceased to be badged as either Austin or Morris.

The final development of the Maxi was the Maxi 2 model of 1980, which was only a very minor cosmetic facelift although it marked the end of the 1500 model. The 1.7 model in L, HL and twin-carb HLS forms continued in production until July 1981, its demise being perhaps more genuinely mourned than that of any other discontinued Austin car of the Leyland period.

Specifications

MAXI 1500 1969-79
Engine four cylinder ohc transverse, 1485cc
Bore × stroke 76.2×81.3mm
Power 74bhp @ 5500rpm
Transmission five-speed manual in engine sump, front wheel drive
Chassis unitary construction
Wheelbase 104in (2642mm)
Length 158.3in (4022mm)
Width 64.1in (1629mm)
Height 55.3in (1404mm)
Weight 2178lbs (988kg)
Suspension independent with interconnected Hydrolastic (Hydragas from 1977)
Brakes hydraulic, discs at front
Bodywork five-door hatchback
Top speed 86mph (138km/h)
Price when introduced £993
Total production 111,370

MAXI 1750/1750L/1750HL SINGLE CARBURETTOR 1970-81
As Maxi 1500, except:
Engine 1748cc
Bore × stroke 76.2×95.8mm
Power 84bhp @ 5000rpm
Transmission automatic optional
Length Maxi 2 1980-81 159.75in (4057mm)
Top speed 89mph (143km/h)
Price when introduced £1102
Total production (including twin carburettor models) 360,728

MAXI 1750HL/HLS TWIN CARBURETTOR 1972-81
As Maxi 1750, except:
Power 93bhp @ 5350rpm
Transmission manual only
Top speed 97mph (156km/h)
Price when introduced £1392

Left The heavily-revised 'Mark III' Mini of 1969 was fitted with wind-down windows and internal door hinges, and was no longer an Austin or Morris, just a Mini.

Below The Clubman driver at least had the instruments directly in front, but they were quite some way down there and very small. Destined for a European market, this left-hand drive model had a laminated windscreen and hazard warning flashers before they became commonplace on home market models.

Right How the PR people work out that a particular car is the X millionth is a bit of a mystery. Anyway, somebody thought this event was worth celebrating. The chosen car was one of the new Mini Clubman models with the squared-up front end.

Mini 1969 to date

The facelifted Mini was introduced at the 1969 Motor Show. There was not a great deal of difference externally and it would take a keen eye to spot that the door hinges were now internal, while the sliding windows had been replaced by conventional wind-down ones. In fact the bodyshell had been almost totally re-jigged and re-designed, justifying the new ADO 20 project number given to the Mini from then on. There was also a reversion from Hydrolastic to dry cone rubber suspension. There were 850 and 1000 saloons as before, as well as van and pick-up versions, and a short-lived Mini-Cooper 'S' Mark III.

While the new Minis were simply Minis, without either Austin or Morris badges (although the Austin badge would briefly re-appear on Minis under the Musgrove regime in the early 1980s!), there was an additional new model which was immediately identifiable by its all-new front end. This was the Mini Clubman, with a squared-up front end adding to the car's overall length, much to the disgust of Sir Alec Issigonis. The new front might have slightly improved the car's performance in a frontal collision but was probably dictated by fashion more than anything else. The Clubman was fitted with the 998cc engine and was available in saloon or estate car form (there was no longer an estate version of the ordinary Mini). The Clubman bodyshell was also used for the new 1275 GT model, which had a single-carburettor 1275 cc engine and was never quite the successor to the Cooper 'S' that Leyland might have hoped for, although they did sell a lot more of them. While the Clubman estate had the dry suspension from the start, the saloon and the 1275 GT stuck to Hydrolastic until 1971.

In the rather lacklustre early 1970s the Mini established itself as the best-selling British Leyland car, worldwide production topping 300,000 cars in 1971 and 1972 and not dropping below 200,000 until 1978. But these figures, impressive though they were, were to a degree only a reflection on the relative lack of success of newer models such as the Maxi and the Allegro. The only other Leyland best-seller in those years was the uninspired Morris Marina. The Mini went through the 1970s with precious little in the way of development, and once the Mini-Cooper had finally gone in mid-1971 (except for certain models made abroad) the model range was left unaltered until 1980 when the Clubman saloon and 1275 GT were discontinued.

Minis continued to be made in Australia, where the Moke became Australia's own Mini (although it later transplanted to Portugal and then Italy). The Belgian assembly plant at Seneffe contributed large numbers of Minis, some fitted with 1098cc engines and known as Mini Specials. Innocenti in Italy continued to make Minis including the Mini-Cooper 1300 until 1974, when they brought out the 'New Mini', an attractive Bertone-designed hatchback which used Mini mechanical components but subsequently received a Japanese three-cylinder Daihatsu engine. AUTHI, the British Leyland operation in Spain, made Minis, and also had a Mini-Cooper model in its range.

The golden days of the Mini in motor sports were largely over by 1970 but one driver, Richard Longman, with sponsorship from Birmingham-based Leyland dealers the Patrick Motors Group, gave the Mini a remarkable comeback in saloon car racing in 1977-78. He became the first driver to win Group 1 races outright in a Mini, at Donington and Brands Hatch in 1977, and with his 1275 GT became the British saloon car champion in 1978.

With the coming of the Metro in

From 1969 onwards, the estate car always had the Clubman front end. On later cars, even the single remaining fake wood trim strip gave way to contrast-colour tape striping.

With its tamer single carburettor engine the Mini 1275 GT was not quite the successor to the Mini-Cooper 'S' that British Leyland publicists wanted you to believe – but it sold in far greater numbers.

The 1979 20th anniversary 1100 Special limited edition (they made 5100) was devised at a time when vinyl roofs and tape schemes were considered the answer to the marketing department's prayers. The alloy wheels and 1098cc engine were possibly more relevant.

1980 the Mini range was pruned. The Clubman saloon and 1275 GT disappeared in August 1980, the 850 saloon in 1981, and the estate – no longer badged Clubman – was discontinued in early 1982. In 1983 the van and pick-up also went out of production. In effect this left just one model, the Mini 1000 saloon, in two trim levels, originally known as the City and the HL. These became the E and HLE models in 1982, the latter soon being re-named Mayfair to tie in with a rash of other Mayfair models appearing in the Austin range – reviving one of the pre-war Austin model names.

There was also a growing number of 'limited edition' models, sparked off by the 20th anniversary model of 1979, which had a 1098cc engine. The 1983 Sprite had cast-alloy wheels, and the 25th anniversary model in 1984 was the first 'ordinary' Mini to have 12in wheels and front disc brakes, since standardised also on the normal production models. Inevitably there was a 30th anniversary model in 1989, and the rather dramatic ERA-Mini into which was shoe-horned the turbo-charged 1275cc engine from the MG Metro Turbo. It was a conversion job by ERA and made the fastest Mini ever.

In the later 1980s production figures gradually stabilised at around 40,000 cars per year, and the Mini continued to find buyers in the home market as well as in export markets, particularly in France and Germany but also in Japan. A surprise was the reappearance in 1990 of the Mini-Cooper, with a 1275cc engine, first as a limited edition (bearing John Cooper's signature!) but soon after as a standard production model. There was an approved tuning kit which would turn it into a reborn Mini-Cooper 'S'. And after numerous private convertible versions had been carried out by Crayford and others over a 30-year period, the official Mini Convertible was launched in 1991. With more than five million Minis made (the milestone was reached in 1986) the Mini looks set to continue almost indefinitely, despite repeated rumours of its demise.

Specifications

MINI 850 1969-83
Engine four cylinder ohv transverse, 848cc
Bore × stroke 62.9×68.3mm
Power 34bhp @ 5500rpm
Transmission four-speed manual in engine sump (automatic optional on saloon model to 1971), front wheel drive
Chassis unitary construction with subframes

Wheelbase 80.2in (2036mm) saloon; 84.2in (2139mm) van, pick-up
Length 120.25in (3054mm) saloon; 130in (3302mm) van, pick-up
Width 55.5in (1410mm)
Height 53in (1346mm)
Weight 1360lbs (617kg)
Suspension independent with rubber cones front and rear
Brakes hydraulic
Bodywork two-door saloon, van, pick-up
Top speed 70mph (113km/h)
Price when introduced £596 (saloon)
Total production (approximate figures) saloon 407,670 (1970-81), van 94,899 (1970-83), pick-up 12,130 (1970-80)

MINI 1000 1969 to date
As Mini 850, except:
Engine 998cc
Bore × stroke 64.6×76.2mm
Power 38bhp @ 5250rpm
Transmission automatic optional on saloon model
Brakes discs at front from 1984
Bodywork two-door saloon, van, pick-up
Top speed 77mph (124km/h)
Price when introduced £675 (saloon)
Total production (approximate figures) saloon 1,421,622 (1970 to end of 1990), van 82,356 (1970-83), pick-up 15,397 (1970-83)

MINI 1100 SPECIAL 1977-81
As Mini 1000, except:
Engine 1098cc
Bore × stroke 64.6×83.7mm

Below A nice new chunky steering wheel did more for the Mini Mayfair interior than the old triple-instrument pack from the 1275GT.

Left A 1985 Mini – the 'Ritz' limited edition – showing the new 12 inch wheels which accompanied the introduction of disc brakes in 1984, and also proving that by then Minis did once again carry the Austin name!

Right TV personality Noel Edmonds drives the 5,000,000th Mini off the line in 1986. The impressive total production figure did include a generous allowance for Minis produced overseas.

Right Compared to earlier Longbridge assembly shots, some modernisation of the CAB facility is apparent in this 1989 photo. The car is a 'Flame', yet another Mini limited edition, its white roof copied from the original Mini-Cooper.

Power 45bhp @ 5250rpm
Transmission manual only
Bodywork two-door saloon
Total production 78,853
This model was predominantly manufactured at Seneffe in Belgium for sale in European markets, the only UK-made version being the 20th Anniversary Limited Edition model of 1979, 5100 made. In 1977-79 there was also a 1275cc engined 1300 special, made only for export, total production 31,360

MINI CLUBMAN 1969-82
As Mini 1000, except:
Engine 998cc (1098cc on some manual gearbox models 1975-80)
Wheelbase 84.2in (2139mm) on estate car
Length 124.6in (3165mm) saloon; 133.9in (3400mm) estate car
Weight 1406lbs (639kg) saloon, 1514lbs (687kg) estate car
Suspension Hydrolastic until 1971, rubber cones thereafter
Bodywork two-door saloon, estate car
Top speed 74mph (119km/h)
Price when introduced £720 (saloon), £763 (estate car)
Total production (approximate figures) saloon 275,583 (1970-80), estate car 197,606 (1970-82)

In 1980 when the saloon was discontinued, the estate car was re-badged as 'Mini 1000HL'

MINI 1275GT 1969-80
As Mini Clubman, except:
Engine 1275cc
Bore × stroke 70.6×81.3mm
Power 60bhp @ 5250rpm
Transmission manual only
Weight 1504lbs (683kg)
Brakes discs at front
Bodywork saloon only
Top speed 87mph (140km/h)
Price when introduced £834
Total production 110,673

ERA MINI TURBO 1989 to date
Engine four cylinder ohv transverse turbocharged, 1275cc
Bore × stroke 70.6×81.3mm
Power 96bhp @ 6130rpm
Transmission four-speed manual in engine sump, front wheel drive
Chassis unitary construction with subframes
Wheelbase 80.2in (2036mm)
Length 120.5in (3060mm)
Width 55.5in (1410mm)
Height 52.4in (1331mm)
Weight 1624lbs (737kg)

Suspension independent with rubber cones front and rear
Brakes hydraulic, discs at front
Bodywork two-door saloon
Top speed 110mph (177km/h)
Price when introduced £12,000
Production to end of 1990, 302

NEW MINI-COOPER 1990 to date
Engine four cylinder ohv transverse, 1275cc
Bore × stroke 70.6×81.3mm
Power 61bhp @ 5550rpm
Transmission four-speed manual in engine sump, front wheel drive
Chassis unitary construction with subframes
Wheelbase 80.1in (2035mm)
Length 120.25in (3054mm)
Width 55.5in (1410mm)
Height 53.25in (1353mm)
Weight 1530lbs (695kg)
Suspension independent with rubber cones front and rear
Brakes hydraulic, discs at front
Bodywork two-door saloon
Top speed 92mph (148km/h)
Price when introduced £6995
Production to end of 1990, 6441
From late 1991, the original carburettor-engined model was replaced by a fuel-injection version

Leyland's home-made dumpling also known as the Austin Allegro. This one is an 1100 de-luxe two-door. In other words, the absolutely most basic model!

One improvement, at least, over the 1100/1300 range was the much more accessible engine – still the faithful old A-series on lesser models. The radiator was now front-mounted.

The most controversial fitment of the original Allegro was this 'Quartic' steering wheel. The facia design broke new ground for Leyland. This is one of the more basic models, with simple instrumentation and a four-speed gearbox.

Allegro 1973-1982

The Allegro is as redolent of the 1970s as is Kojak's catchphrase (remember *him?*), "Who loves ya, baby?" Someone, somewhere evidently loves the Allegro; last I heard they were forming an owners' club. *Car* magazine loved it too, when it first came out; but they have tried to make you forget that ever since.

It does rather beggar belief that in the year Britain joined the Common Market British Leyland launched the Allegro as their car for Europe. Fair enough, it was a more 'European' car than the lacklustre Marina; on the other hand, it came so much later than the Citroën GS and the Alfasud that you would have thought *somebody* at Longbridge would have been aware of

the benchmark European cars in the Allegro class at the time when the successor to the 1100/1300 range was being developed. In 1974, to make matters worse, Volkswagen brought out the Golf. The Allegro never had a chance.

Development of the Allegro only began after the BMC-Leyland merger in 1968, when Harry Webster arrived from Triumph at Canley to take over Alec Issigonis's responsibility as chief engineer. It became corporate policy to develop both conventional cars (which would be labelled Morris) and advanced cars, which would be labelled Austin. The first tangible evidence of this was the Morris Marina. By 1971, the need for a successor to the 1100-1300 range was becoming pressing. Ford had launched the Escort in 1968 and the Cortina Mark III in 1970, while neither the Hillman Avenger nor the Vauxhall Viva could be disregarded. The new car, code-named ADO 67, was styled in house at Longbridge, the first major work for Leyland's young stylist Harris Mann. In engineering terms, the Allegro followed previous BMC practice, with transverse

engine, gearbox in the sump and front wheel drive. The old A-series engines from the 1100 and 1300 models were carried forward, but to reinforce Austin's position further up the market, the Maxi E-series engines of 1500 and 1750cc were also fitted to the new model, complete with five-speed gearboxes. Automatic gearboxes were available on the 1300 and 1500 versions.

So far, so good. There was a new hydro-pneumatic suspension system for the new car, again developed by Alex Moulton and made by Dunlop. It was called Hydragas, and differed from Hydrolastic in that the rubber cones of the earlier system had been replaced by balls containing pressurised nitrogen. These took over the role of shock absorbing, but the actual springing medium was still the interconnected fluid chambers as before. In fact Hydragas worked quite well but the lack of any self-levelling mechanism meant that heavily-laden Allegros ended up dragging their tails.

The styling of the Allegro was certainly different, its dumpy rounded lines being in total contrast to the Giugiaro-inspired 'folded paper' school

Above 'Hottest' of the range was the E-series engined 1750 Sport Special, at first called the SS model. The roof is vinyl-covered and those wheeltrims are plastic.

Above The Allegro 3, here in 1.5HL form, also had a new boot lid pressing and matt black window frames.

which was gaining ground elsewhere in the industry. Unfortunately most people did not consider it attractive. The boot was bigger than on the 1100, but awkward to load, and there was less interior room than on the superseded model. One of the quirks of the original Allegro was the 'quartic' steering wheel, apparently an attempt by Rover stylist David Bache at squaring the circle. It was dropped within a couple of years in favour of an ordinary round steering wheel. The biggest error of judgment was probably that the Allegro was not made as a hatchback, a style becoming tremendously popular for small cars throughout Europe, but presumably Leyland felt they had burnt their fingers sufficiently with the Maxi.

An Allegro estate car followed in 1975, in two-door form only and with equally strange styling which gave it the look of a miniature hearse. Badge-engineering was no longer in favour, but there was still one up-market derivative of the Allegro, the Vanden Plas 1500. The only new panel was the bonnet, which incorporated a rather gothic version of the Vanden Plas

radiator grille. Interior appointments were in the Vanden Plas tradition, with armrests, picnic tables, a wooden facia and leather upholstery. It remained a somewhat limited production model.

As far as Europe was concerned, Leyland put the Allegro into the new Belgian assembly plant at Seneffe, from where substantial numbers were even exported to England (presumably when Longbridge went on strike). There was also a short-lived Italian Innocenti version known as the Regent – one would have thought that Allegro would have been the perfect name in Italy, but apparently not. It was not well received in Italy and did not survive de Tomaso's takeover of Innocenti in 1976. Europe greeted the Allegro with indifference.

The Allegro 2 was introduced at the 1975 Motor Show but you would be hard put to spot the differences, and the Allegro 3 followed in 1979, with new radiator grilles, bumpers and boot lid. In late 1980 the 1100 (or 1.1) was replaced by a 998cc engined 1.0 model. Meanwhile there had been an attempt to jazz up the Allegro's dowdy image with the 'Equipe' limited edition model

The most extensive facelift came late in life for the Allegro, the Allegro 3 featuring a much simplified grille, black bumpers and a chin spoiler, and some wheeltrims that were supposed to look like cast-alloy wheels. The estate car styling was even odder than that of the saloon.

of 1979. This had the 1750 engine in a two-door body, cast-alloy wheels and a silver/black colour scheme with a rather overwhelming arrangement of red and orange tape along the sides and up the rear quarter pillars.

After the launch of the Metro in 1980, and with the new model beginning to take sales away from the Allegro as well as the Mini, the Allegro was only just being kept going until BL's next new model, the LC10 Maestro, was ready. After having lingered for some time, it passed away quietly in its tenth year. There were no mourners at the graveside.

The interior of the Vanden Plas version was in keeping with the best Vanden Plas traditions, and was a vast improvement over the ordinary Allegro's.

The radiator grille of the Vanden Plas 1500 was at least distinctive but has earned this model the unflattering sobriquet of 'Noddycar'. It seems less at home in front of Blenheim Palace than the two Daimler Vanden Plas models flanking it.

Specifications

ALLEGRO 1100/1.1 1973-80
Engine four cylinder ohv transverse, 1098cc
Bore × stroke 64.6×83.7mm
Power 49bhp @ 5250rpm
Transmission four-speed manual in engine sump, front wheel drive
Chassis unitary construction
Wheelbase 96.1in (2442mm)
Length 151.7in (3852mm)
Width 63.5in (1613mm)
Height 55in (1398mm)
Weight approx 1850lbs (840kg)
Suspension independent with interconnected Hydragas
Brakes hydraulic, discs at front
Bodywork two-door saloon, four-door saloon
Top speed 82mph (132km/h)
Price when introduced £973-£1009
Total production 136,380

ALLEGRO 1300/1.3 1973-82
As 1100/1.1 model, except:
Engine 1275cc
Bore × stroke 70.6×81.3mm
Power 59bhp @ 5300rpm
Transmission automatic optional
Length (estate car) 155.2in (3942mm)
Height (estate car) 55.8in (1417mm)
Weight approx 1900lbs (863kg), estate car 2000lbs (908kg)

Bodywork also estate car
Top speed 83mph (134km/h)
Price when introduced £1009-£1093, estate car (1975) £1908
Total production 312,467 saloons, 37,202 estate cars

ALLEGRO 1500/1.5 1973-82
As 1300/1.3 model, except:
Engine four cylinder ohc transverse, 1485cc
Bore × stroke 76.2×81.3mm
Power 72bhp @ 5500rpm
Transmission five-speed manual in engine sump, automatic optional
Weight approx 1950lbs (885kg), estate car 2050lbs (931kg)
Top speed 84mph (135km/h)
Price when introduced £1164-£1277, estate car (1975) £2056
Total production 107,082 saloons, 20,172 estate cars (incl. 1.7 estate auto). (NB: Two-door saloons only offered 1973-74. In the Allegro 3 range, 1979-83, the 1500 automatic was replaced by 1.7 automatic with single carburettor 1750 engine)

ALLEGRO 1750/1.7 1973-82
As 1500/1.5 model, except:
Engine 1748cc
Bore × stroke 76.2×95.8mm
Power 80bhp @ 5000rpm (single carb), 91bhp @ 5250rpm (twin carb)
Transmission manual only (except

Allegro 3, 1979-83, when automatic optional on single carb model)
Weight approx 2000lbs (908kg)
Bodywork four-door saloon; two-door saloon 1973-74 only, and 'Equipe' limited edition model 1979; estate car, 1979-83 only, 1.7 single carb automatic
Top speed 94mph (151km/h)
Price when introduced £1254-£1367, Equipe (1979) £4360
Total production 20,801 saloons

ALLEGRO 3 1.0 1980-82
As 1100/1.1 model, except:
Engine 998cc
Bore × stroke 64.6×76.3mm
Power 44bhp @ 5250rpm
Weight approx 1800lbs (817kg)
Total production 8,246

VANDEN PLAS 1500 (1.5/1.7) 1974-80
As Allegro 1500, except:
Power 68bhp @ 5500rpm (single carb), 77bhp @ 5750rpm (twin carb)
Length 154.25in (3918mm)
Weight approx 2100lbs (953kg)
Price when introduced £1950
Total production 11,842
(NB: In 1979 1500 automatic replaced by 1.7 automatic with single carb 1748cc engine, 72bhp @ 4900rpm. 1500 manual with single carb replaced by 1.5 manual with twin carbs)

18-22 series, Princess and Ambassador 1975-1984

To produce one unsuccessful car may be regarded as a misfortune, but to produce two smacks of carelessness. So what are we to make of British Leyland who managed to lay three eggs in a row – the Maxi, the Allegro and the Princess?

The intentions behind ADO 71, sometime also code-named 'Diablo', were as good as always. Produce a stylish and up-to-date car with all the advantages of the old 1800/2200 range in terms of generous interior accommodation, but with a much more luxurious specification to placate those customers who had shied away from the basic, indeed spartan, interior furnishings and style of the old 'land crab'. As in case of the Allegro, the existing 1800 and 2200 engines were carried forward from the old model to the new, and the Hydragas suspension first seen on the Allegro was also found on the new bigger car.

It was in terms of styling that British Leyland managed to surprise us. ADO 71, like the Allegro, came from Harris Mann's drawing board, in his 'wedge' period. The front end was long and low, and the waistline climbed steadily

towards the truncated fastback tail of the car. The effect was quite striking and the whole ensemble was aesthetically far more successful than the Allegro. But it was still not everybody's cup of tea, a fact tacitly admitted by British Leyland who subsequently advertised the Princess as "Not a car for Mr Average". Mr Average took a good look and went off to buy another Cortina. Unkind critics said that the Princess looked much better if there was a load in the boot, as additional weight on the rear made the car drag its tail (thanks to the Hydragas suspension) which balanced the looks wonderfully well.

Above This was the original line-up of the 18-22 Series as launched in March 1975. Three Austins, with trapezoidal headlamps; three Morrises, with double round headlamps; and the single Wolseley right out in front.

Below The profile of the Princess was quite unmistakeable. To camouflage the worst of the tail-high stance, the photographer had this car run uphill past the camera, and there was probably some weight in the boot, too.

The '2000 HL' badge proves this to be a Princess 2 of 1978. The wheel trims resembling finned brake drums were characteristic of the up-market Princess models.

The interior, at least on the HLS model (which replaced the Wolseley), was quite well finished by mid-70s standards. This is a Princess 2 but there were only ever detail differences between the various models.

Launched as "The car that's got it all together" in the spring of 1975, the new 18-22 series was generally well received by a press which was already becoming somewhat jaded about British Leyland. The only thing it had not got together was the naming and marketing philosophy. Originally there were Austin, Morris and Wolseley versions of the new car, the Wolseley only in a super-de-luxe form with the six-cylinder engine, the Austins and Morrises with either four- or six-cylinder engines and more basic trim. The Austins had trapezoidal head-lamps, the Morris and Wolseley models twin round headlamps. The Morris and Wolseley also had different-shaped bonnets and radiator grilles, the Wolseley still with that marque's traditional lit-up badge.

But within six months the three individual marque names were swept aside in favour of a new much simplified range under the joint name Princess. It is debatable whether this was a direct result of a recommendation in the Ryder report; it is more likely that someone at British Leyland saw the marketing sense in making a simpler range of cars under one brand name which could then be sold through either Austin or Morris franchises. All Princess models had the original Austin-style bonnet and radiator grille, the twin round headlamps now denoting the four-cylinder 1800 and 1800 HL models, the trapezoidal lamps being the preserve of the 2200 HL and HLS.

Unfortunately the Princess fell victim to increasingly poor build quality, with numerous stories circulating in workshops, showrooms, saloon bars and the motoring press. It was difficult to sell a Princess second-hand or even to trade it in at a Leyland dealership. A well-publicised problem concerning the drive shafts on the manual-gearbox 2200 model added further fuel to the fire, this model being actually taken out of production for some months, while Leyland made the best of a bad job by selling the 2200 automatic as a 'limited edition' model badged as the 'Special Six'.

In 1978 the old B-series 1800 engine was replaced in the Princess 2 by the new overhead-camshaft O-series engines, in 1700 and 2000 form, while the 2200 six-cylinder model continued at the top of the range. Apart from new style badges there was not a great amount of external difference. Behind the scenes, however, the design and engineering departments at Longbridge were busily working on a much more important improvement – turning the Princess into a hatchback.

This project was marked by a lack of direction. At first it was simply the intention to cut a rear door into the car, with the minimum of structural alteration. Then the powers that be gradually relented and week by week allowed the stylists to change one more panel, then another panel and so on. At the end of the day the face-lifted car emerged with only the front doors being carried over without change, yet because the lines through the door dictated the remainder of the design, the new, almost totally re-skinned car ended up looking virtually just like a Princess. Then there was some wrangling over the name: the possibility of reviving Wolseley was mooted, then Austin Westminster was under consideration, finally Austin Ambassador was pulled out of the hat.

The Ambassador was launched in 1982, in 1.7- and 2.0-litre forms. The six-cylinder engine had been dropped, but there was a special luxury version of the 2-litre model bearing the Vanden Plas name tag. Apart from the tailgate and folding rear seat, the Ambassador also had additional quarter-lights in the rear pillars, and an all-new front end with a backwards-sloping radiator grille and square headlamps which came from the Morris Ital. The front

The facia was totally up-to-date, with mod cons such as a digital clock and electric windows. The 'econometer' in the instrument pack was a gadget not repeated on subsequent Austin models. This is the Vanden Plas model.

wings were new, as was the windscreen, the roof was largely re-designed and re-engineered, the rear doors were re-skinned, and the tail panel and rear lights were new. With a little more forethought and planning Leyland could have had a whole new car for the money.

Truth was it was only a stop-gap before the new LM11 or Montego model could be introduced. After only two years, the Ambassador faded unobtrusively away.

Specifications

PRINCESS 1800, 1800HL 1975-78
Engine four cylinder ohv transverse, 1798cc
Bore × stroke 80.3×88.9mm
Power 82bhp @ 5250rpm
Transmission four-speed manual in engine sump (automatic optional), front wheel drive
Chassis unitary construction
Wheelbase 105in (2667mm)
Length 175.35in (4454mm)
Width 67.8in (1723mm)
Height 55.5in (1409mm)
Weight 2557lbs (1160kg)
Suspension independent with interconnected Hydragas
Brakes hydraulic, discs at front
Bodywork four-door saloon
Top speed 96mph (154km/h)
Price when introduced £2117-£2215
Total production 84,867

PRINCESS 2200HL, 2200HLS 1975-82
As 1800 models, except:
Engine six cylinder ohc transverse, 2227cc
Bore × stroke 76.2×81.3mm
Power 110bhp @ 5250rpm
Weight 2638lbs (1197kg), HLS 2677lbs (1215kg)
Top speed 104mph (167km/h)
Price when introduced £2424-£2838
Total production 63,443

PRINCESS 2 1700L, 1700HL 1978-82
As 1800 models, except:
Engine four cylinder ohc transverse, 1695cc
Bore × stroke 84.5×76mm
Power 88bhp @ 5200rpm
Wheelbase 105.25in (2673mm)
Length 175.4in (4456mm)
Width 68.1in (1730mm)
Weight 2390lbs (1085kg)
Top speed 98mph (158km/h)
Price when introduced £3725-£3980
Total production 41,134

PRINCESS 2 2000HL 1978-82
As 1700 models, except:
Engine 1994cc
Bore × stroke 84.5×89mm
Power 92bhp @ 4900rpm
Weight 2400lbs (1090kg)
Top speed 98mph (158km/h)
Price when introduced £4059-£4385
Total production 35,498

AMBASSADOR 1.7L, 1.7HL 1982-84
As Princess 2 1700, except:
Length 179.3in (4554mm)
Weight 2639lbs (1198kg)
Bodywork five-door hatchback
Top speed 98mph (158km/h)
Price when introduced £5105-£6432
Total production 24,989

AMBASSADOR 2.0HL 1982-84
As Ambassador 1.7 models, except:
Engine 1994cc
Bore × stroke 84.5×89mm
Power 92bhp @ 4900rpm
Weight 2653lbs (1204kg)
Top speed 101mph (163km/h)
Price when introduced £6108-£6757
Total production 18,438 (including HLS and Vanden Plas models)

AMBASSADOR 2.0HLS, VANDEN PLAS 1982-84
As Ambassador 2.0HL, except:
Power 100bhp @ 5250rpm
Weight 2741lbs (1244kg)
Top speed 104mph (167km/h)
Price when introduced £6917-£8404
Total production see 2.0HL

Above Getting it wrong, first time. Under all the camouflage is one of the ADO88 prototypes which so offended Michael Edwardes with their spartan functionality.

Right At long last, a small hatchback from Longbridge! The Metro, here in 1.3HLS guise, was a genuinely practical little car, as well as nicely finished and equipped.

Above Austin's success story of the 1980s. The production Metro looked much better than any Austin for a decade but was also a much more mainstream design.

Metro 1980-1990

Replacing the Mini was a long drawn-out and painful process, not assisted by the fact that the British Leyland company was effectively nationalised in 1975 and became increasingly subject to public scrutiny, while a new generation of motoring journalists were only too ready to take and publish 'scoop' photographs of prototype cars they might encounter on the road. The internal company debate was mostly over whether to replace the Mini with a similarly-sized car, or whether to develop a slightly bigger car to compete against the growing number of super-Minis, of which the Ford Fiesta was the most important in the British market.

By 1977 the debate had been resolved in favour of project ADO88. This was a slightly bigger car than the Mini, brilliantly well packaged in the best Issigonis tradition, but with rather basic styling inside and out, suggesting that it was aimed at the economy/utility end of the market. The styling was the car's undoing – it earned bad marks when subjected to customer clinics. Then Michael Edwardes came in as BL chairman, and asked for a quick restyling job. The Longbridge studio

Much of the Metro investment went into the new body plant at Longbridge's West Works, opened by none other than HRH The Prince of Wales. Much of the welding was done by robots.

under Harris Mann responded within a matter of weeks, producing the revised styling for what became known as the LC8 project, and which became the Metro we all know.

Of course it was originally the Mini-Metro, launched to much ballyhoo at the 1980 Motor Show. A small three-door hatchback, its packaging allowed it to offer as much inside room as most competitors up to a foot longer, although the boot was smallish. Engines were

of 1 or 1.3 litres, now called the A-plus series, with four-speed gearboxes in the sump, following the Mini lay-out. Suspension was an improved version of the Hydragas system. The car still suffered from some of the classic Mini shortcomings, such as the inconvenient driving position and noisy intermediate gears, and the absence of a five-speed gearbox would come to be increasingly remarked upon as the years went by. An automatic version

Above The van version of the Metro, created by the simple expedient of blanking out the rear side windows and omitting the rear seat.

Left This ghosted view of the Metro emphasizes the passenger accommodation and boot space – which were indeed remarkable for its size.

Above Not all diehards appreciated the MG Metro but it became the best-selling of all MG saloons and marked the welcome return of a famous badge in 1982.

was not at first offered, and when it did appear the Metro 1.3 automatic was a model in its own right. (The Mini part of the name was dropped after the first few years.)

Michael Edwardes was much to the forefront at the Metro launch, as was his appointee as managing director of the unhandily-titled BL Cars Light/Medium division (soon to be re-named Austin Rover Group), one Harold Musgrove, an old Austin apprentice who had risen through the ranks and was now one of the most ebullient and straight-talking managers in the motor industry. Hailed as BL's 'make-or-break' car, the Metro was shown on TV commercials repelling an invasion of foreign cars on the cliffs of Dover. (It was conveniently overlooked that the first co-operative agreement between BL and Honda had been signed not long before).

Make no mistake, the Metro was a very good car, better than the uninspired Austin family cars of the 1970s. It took a while before the model range was shaken down and established (such variations as the 1.3 S and the HLS model did not last long), and in 1982 a luxury-equipped Vanden Plas version was launched, together with the more sporting MG-badged derivative. Later in the same year, the

ultimate high-performance Metro was introduced, the MG Metro Turbo. The two MG versions always accounted for a substantial proportion of Metro sales.

In the marketplace the Metro did better than any other BL car for a long time. While it took substantial sales away from the Mini, it also made inroads in Allegro territory. It was always in the top ten but rarely in the number one spot, and it usually had to play second fiddle in its class after the Ford Fiesta. Useful numbers were exported, and the Metro helped to raise awareness of British cars in such important markets as France, Italy and Germany. The most famous Metro customer was a shy young nursery teacher in London. Her name was Lady

The MG Metros had quite the nicest interiors of all Metros. This is the Turbo version, with appropriate steering wheel logo and a boost gauge. The instrument pack was particularly nicely designed.

Diana Spencer.

By 1984 half-a-million Metros had been made, the event being duly celebrated with a limited edition model called the VP 500, based on the Vanden Plas but with the added luxury of full leather trim. More mundanely, a Metro van had also made its appearance, being little more than a saloon with blanked-out rear side windows and no rear seat. This was at one stage badged Morris! At the 1984 Motor Show, the 'Mark II' version of the Metro took its bow. This was face-lifted with a new front end and a new facia, and for the first time a five-door Metro became available. The Vanden Plas model was now only available in five-door form, with the option of an automatic

The 1984 Metro Mark II had a re-designed front end, and a five-door version was introduced. The original Vanden Plas had been a three-door but from then on it became a five-door only.

The second-generation MG models retained the three-door configuration but also had the revised front end, and new cast-alloy wheels.

gearbox. The most basic model was the Metro City, while the Metro Mayfair was an intermediate trim level. There was a good spread of three- and five-door models with either 1- or 1.3-litre engines at various trim levels, but the two MG versions continued in three-door form only.

The cars' popularity in the marketplace was undiminished, and with only occasional adjustments to the model mix the Metro continued in production until 1990. There were the inevitable limited editions along the way, usually offering additional equipment and trim at an attractive price, and given a catchy name such as 'Advantage', 'Moritz', 'Surf' or 'Red Hot' and 'Jet Black'. Even the old Mini-name 'Clubman' was revived for a Metro variation. Towards the end of production, the GT-a and Sport models of 1989 offered MG-style performance and trim at a lower cost, but of course without the added cachet of the octagon badge. A Metro was the ten millionth car built at Longbridge.

Metros lost the Austin name in 1987 and existed in a nameless limbo for some three years. In April 1990 most Metros were replaced by the new Rover Metro (Rover 100-series in export markets) with the new K-series engine, but despite an extensive face-lift the new model was still recognisably a descendant of the Austin Metro. Of the original range, the van and automatic versions continued in production for a few more months.

Specification

METRO 1.0 1980 to date
Engine four cylinder ohv transverse, 998cc
Bore × stroke 64.6×76.2mm
Power 44bhp @ 5250rpm
Transmission four-speed manual in engine sump, front wheel drive
Chassis unitary construction
Wheelbase 88.6in (2251mm)
Length 134.1in (3405mm)
Width 60.9in (1549mm)
Height 53.6in (1361mm)
Weight 1638-1679lbs (743-762kg) 3-door, 1653lbs (750kg) van, 1798lbs (816kg) 5-door
Suspension independent Hydragas
Brakes hydraulic, discs at front
Bodywork three-door hatchback (1980-90), five-door hatchback (1984-90), van (1982 to date)
Top speed 85mph (137km/h)
Price when introduced 3-door (1980) £3095-£3695, 5-door (1984) £4473-£4872
Total production 3-door 777,391 (1980-90); 5-door 141,385 (1984-90); van 30,117 (1982 to end of 1990)

METRO 1.3 1980 to date
As 1.0, except:
Engine 1275cc
Bore × stroke 70.6×81.3mm
Power 63bhp @ 5650rpm (MG 72bhp @ 6000rpm; Turbo 93bhp @ 6130rpm)
Transmission automatic optional (MG models manual only)
Weight 1662-1867lbs (754-847kg) 3-door; 1816-1904lbs (824-864kg) 5-door
Top speed 94mph (151km/h), MG 1300 100mph (161km/h), MG Turbo 110mph (177km/h)
Price when introduced 3-door (1980) £3995-£4296, MG 1300 (1982) £4799, Vanden Plas 3-door (1982) £4995, MG Turbo (1982) £5650, 5-door (1984) £5389-£5985
Total production 3-door 261,213 (1980-90); 5-door 119,630 (1984-90); van 8,825 (1982 to end of 1990); Vanden Plas 3-door 15,739 (1982-84); Vanden Plas 5-door 19,700 (1984-89); MG 1300 120,197 (1982-90); MG Turbo 21,968 (1984-89)
After the introduction of the Rover Metro in 1990, only the following models remained in production: 1.3 3-door automatic and 1.0 and 1.3 vans.

In the Austin hierarchy of the 1980s the Vanden Plas badge denoted the most luxurious version, and so it was with the Maestro range. Still with some Allegro overtones, the styling was a neater and more workmanlike job.

The original Maestro facia – here in a non-talking, non-digital version – was of rather uncompromising design and often suffered from badly fitting panels. It was eventually replaced by the one-piece moulding from the Montego.

Maestro 1983 to date

I once had this girlfriend named Nicolette. Ours was not exactly what you might call a passionate relationship, in fact it was never consummated, but she would always come out in the car with me. Proper backseat driver she was, constantly nagging me in hectoring tones, telling me to put my seat belt on or that I had left the lights on, or that my fuel was low; even, on one occasion, triumphantly, that the fuel was used. I wished I could shut her up. I used to think that the car meant more to her than I did, and I was proved right: when I changed the car she calmly went off with the new owner. Still, I was quite relieved to see the back of her. – Nicolette (full name Nicolette McKenzie) was the synthesized voice coming out of the facia in my Maestro.

More than anything else it was this one gimmick which caught the public's imagination when the Maestro was launched in 1983. It was a soon-discarded option which came with the all-electronic digital instrument display on the Vanden Plas and MG versions. Perhaps it distracted rather too much from the fact that the Maestro was quite the best family car under the name of

Austin for a decade. Unfortunately, the Maestro may be remembered chiefly as the car which deserved a better fate.

Originally known as project LC 10, it had at one time been a toss-up whether this or the Metro was going to be launched first, only resolved when the larger car ran into a styling crisis which delayed it somewhat. Eventually, a styling proposal from David Bache's Solihull studio was chosen over that made by Harris Mann at Longbridge. The preferred style was described by one wag as "by Allegro out of Rover" and it certainly shared some of the Allegro proportions, but the belt line groove was a David Bache trademark ever since the Rover SD1. Never a contender in the beauty stakes, the Maestro had a certain honest functionalism about it, like a latter-day Austin 1800.

In engineering terms the Maestro

was a departure from traditional Austin practice. Firstly, it had the gearbox on the end of the engine rather than in the sump. The gearboxes were bought in from Volkswagen, and both four- and five-speed versions were available. Secondly, instead of Hydragas the Maestro had simple coil spring suspension, McPherson struts at the front with a light trailing axle at the back, somewhat in the manner of the VW Golf. Only a five-door saloon was available, a three-door version being dropped at a late stage. The engines were the well-tried 1.3-litre A-plus and a new overhead-camshaft 1.6, the R-series, which was developed from the old E-series found in the Maxi and Allegro models. The usual wide variety of trim levels was offered, including a 1.6 Vanden Plas model and an MG version with a twin Weber carburettor version of the 1.6 engine. There was

The original MG Maestro had the 1.6 engine with twin Weber carburettors, replaced in 1984 by this 2-litre fuel-injected model, which at first still had the cast-alloy wheels from the 1.6, as seen here.

The basic Maestros had ordinary bumpers instead of the one-piece plastic mouldings common to the rest of the range (which were only too prone to cracking!).

also a rather ill-judged economy model, the 1.3 HLE, with a special four-speed gearbox where fourth was an overdrive ratio.

The Maestro range was generally given a good reception, but if Austin Rover had hoped that the new model would offer serious competition to the well-established Ford Escort, they were to be disappointed. Like the Metro, the Maestro was a fundamentally good car, but in the early years build quality was suspect and the advanced electronic engine management system was a cause of frequent break-downs. One Austin Rover employee described his early Maestro as "a rattling good car", with the stress on rattling. Build quality would improve, and the electronics did become more reliable, but not before the Maestro had been reduced to an also-ran in the marketplace.

After little more than one year in production the R-series was replaced by the S-series engine first seen in the Montego. Soon afterwards the uncom-promisingly square facia of the Maestro was replaced by the more rounded Montego design, and the 1.6 MG Maestro was replaced by a fuel-injected two-litre model with a five-speed Honda gearbox, again following the lines of the MG Montego. This was the only two-litre petrol Maestro and would establish a devoted following as one of the best GTI-type cars, offering a top speed of almost 115 mph.

A Maestro van was introduced at the 1984 Motor Show and in 1986 was the first model of the range to receive a diesel engine, developed jointly with Perkins. This also appeared in Maestro saloons in 1990. The 1.3 and 1.6 models were still being manufactured, and the 2-litre MG had been joined by a limited-production turbo model from the 1988 Motor Show onwards. But it was by now an open secret that the Maestro only had a limited life expectancy, and the choice of models was drastically reduced when the new Rover 200 series was launched in the autumn of 1989.

Launched with such high hopes only six years before, the Maestro was no longer deemed important enough by Rover to merit even a modest facelift. More or less unchanged, the remaining Maestros – deprived of the Austin name since 1987 – soldiered on in the Rover range in the early 1990s, expected to disappear in 1992. Apart from the ever-green MG model and the van version, the Maestro was only being kept alive because it shared so many parts with the Montego that Rover might as well go on making it...

The only alternative bodystyle for the Maestro was the van, which in 1986 became the first model to be fitted with the Diesel engine.

This D-registered 1987 model year Maestro was one of the last to wear the Austin nameplate.

Specifications

MAESTRO 1.3 1983 to date
Engine four cylinder ohv transverse, 1275cc
Bore × stroke 70.6×81.3mm
Power 68bhp @ 5800rpm (1.3 HLE 64bhp @ 5500rpm)
Transmission four-speed manual end-on (1.3 HLE, 3 + E), five-speed optional, front wheel drive
Chassis unitary construction
Wheelbase 98.7in (2507mm) saloon, 100.5in (2553mm) van
Length 157.5in (4000mm) 1.3 base model, 159.5in (4050mm) other saloons, 171.3in (4351mm) van
Width 66.4in (1687mm) saloons, 67.1in (1704mm) van
Height 56.3in (1429mm) saloons, 63.9in (1623mm) van
Weight 1929-2017lbs (875-915kg) saloons, 2116lbs (960kg) van
Suspension independent strut and coil front, trailing axle with coils rear (saloon), semi-elliptic leaf (van)
Brakes hydraulic, discs at front
Bodywork five-door hatchback, van
Top speed 96mph (154km/h)
Price when introduced £4555-£5345
Production to end of 1990, saloon 292,303, van 64,695

MAESTRO 1.6 1983 to date
As 1.3, except:
Engine four cylinder ohc transverse, 1598cc
Bore × stroke 76.2×87.6mm
Power 81bhp @ 5500rpm (MG: 102bhp @ 6000rpm)
Transmission four- or five-speed, automatic optional (MG five-speed only)
Weight 2083-2172lbs (945-985kg)
Top speed 101mph (163km/h), MG 111mph (179km/h)
Price when introduced £5225-£6245
Production to end of 1990, saloon 110,543; van 592 (1986-88); MG 15,160 (1982-84); Vanden Plas 15,552 (1982-88)

MG MAESTRO 2.0 efi AND TURBO 1984-91 (Turbo 1988-89)
As 1.6, except:
Engine 1994cc
Bore × stroke 84.5×89mm
Power 117bhp @ 5500rpm (Turbo 152bhp @ 5100rpm)
Weight 2293lbs (1040kg), Turbo 2379lbs (1080kg)
Bodywork five-door only
Top speed 114mph (183km/h), Turbo 129mph (208km/h)
Price when introduced £7279, Turbo £12,999
Production to end of 1990, MG efi 27,800, MG Turbo 501 (1988-89)

MAESTRO DIESEL van 1986 to date, saloon 1990 to date
As 1.6, except:
Engine 1994cc Diesel
Bore × stroke 84.5×89mm
Power 60bhp @ 4500rpm
Transmission five-speed only
Weight 2451lbs (1096kg) saloon
Top speed 93mph (150km/h)
Price when introduced £7584-£8874 (saloon)
Production to end of 1990, saloon 4934; van 33,037

The Montego followed a year after the Maestro, using much of the same sheet metal, heavy mouldings being added to the doors as part of the camouflage. This was the basic 1.6 model.

At the other end of the Montego range, the MG version was the first model to use the 2-litre fuel injection engine, denoted by a small 'efi' badge on the rear. Rear spoiler and cast-alloy wheels were part of the MG package, and those unique rear quarterlights are much in evidence.

Montego 1984 to date

The Montego deserves a niche in the history books if only because it was the last new model to be launched bearing the name of Austin – although like its stablemates it lost the Austin name in 1987 and there was at one time a suggestion that it might be re-launched as the Rover 400-series.

Part of Musgrove's masterplan for the Austin Rover company was to launch a range of medium-sized cars based on a common design to replace the entire 1970s generation from Allegro to Ambassador. The first step had been the Maestro or LC10, launched in 1983, a small-medium five-door hatchback. After a year this was followed by LM11, a medium-sized four-door notchback saloon, while the planned LM12, an upmarket five-door hatchback of Montego dimensions or even bigger, remained still-born in favour of Project XX, the joint Rover-Honda car which was introduced as the Rover 800 in 1986.

The styling of the Montego was a difficult process. Contrary to the oft-repeated assertion of *Car* magazine,

the Montego styling committee did meet, and very frequently at that. The problem was that the car was expected to use the Maestro centre section, but the lines of the Maestro were ill-suited to being stretched into an altogether bigger notchback car. During the gestation period of the Montego, David Bache was replaced as director of styling by Roy Axe, who finally hit upon the unique rear quarterlight solution of the Montego. It had the merit at least of being distinctive (if not unique – see Raymond Loewy's 1947 Studebaker coupé). An alternative front end presented less of a problem, and the Montego emerged as a thoroughly conventional-looking car, something which was considered an advantage at a time when Ford had just burnt their fingers rather badly with the jelly-mould Sierra.

Mechanically the Montego was closely based on the Maestro. A 1.3-litre model formed the base of the range, but more important were the 1.6-litre models, with the new S-series engines, and the 2-litre models with a modified version of the O-series engine from the Princess/Ambassador range. Volkswagen gearboxes were

used on the two smaller cars, and a Honda five-speeder on the 2-litre versions. From the start the Montego range embraced Vanden Plas and MG versions, both with 2-litre engines and fuel injection for the MG. The four-door saloon was followed by a rather handsome estate car, introduced at the 1984 Motor Show and available in 1.6- and 2-litre forms including a Vanden Plas model, although an MG-badged estate remained a one-off prototype. Many estate models incorporated a pair of additional rearwards-facing childrens' seats.

An MG Montego Turbo was launched in 1985, commanding respect equally for its performance – with a top speed of more than 125 mph, it was labelled as the fastest MG ever – and for its tricky handling: in common with several other high-performance front wheel drive cars of the period, it suffered from excessive torque steer, although Austin Rover eventually succeeded in curbing its wayward tendencies.

Like the Maestro, the Montego never quite had the expected impact in the marketplace. The 1.6-2 litre class was one of the most fiercely contested, and the problems that Ford experienced

The Montego estate, new at the 1984 Motor Show, was a particularly harmonious design, besides being by far the most capacious and practical hold-all of all Austin Countryman models.

The pleasant and luxurious interior of the Montego Vanden Plas, with leather upholstery and token bits of wood. This is a 1986 model, by which time the fuel-injected 2-litre engine was also used in the Vanden Plas versions.

with customer resistance to the new-fangled styling of the Sierra were mostly to the benefit of Vauxhall, whose attractive new front wheel drive Cavalier was a *succès d'estime* of the 1980s. The Montego was usually relegated to third place in its class.

A 'Mark II' version was launched at the 1988 Motor Show with slight retouches to front and rear ends. The 1.3-litre version was eventually dropped, and the fuel-injection two-litre engine also became available in non-MG badged models, spearheaded by the 2.0 Si which was in effect a civilian version of a model which had been available to Police forces for some time. Later came the GTI version in both saloon and estate car forms, while the Vanden Plas model was also offered with the injection engine before the Vanden Plas version was dropped altogether. A diesel-engined Montego became available, using a turbocharged version of the joint Rover-Perkins 2-litre diesel engine first seen in the Maestro van. Some estate cars were given the old Austin name of Countryman.

However, under the new leadership of Graham Day (from 1986) it became

the declared policy of what was now the Rover Group to call all new models Rover and to gradually move upwards in the marketplace. Graham Day suggested that Rover might become a kind of British equivalent of BMW. This policy was reinforced when in 1988 Rover Group was finally privatised by being sold to British Aerospace, while the co-operation with Honda, initiated by Michael Edwardes almost a decade before, continued, Honda even taking a 20% stake in the Rover Group. Little was done to existing models, and the shape of the future was seen when the joint Rover-Honda project YY was launched as the Rover 200 in the autumn of 1989 (a few months after

the appearance of its Honda Concerto sibling in Japan). This small-medium hatchback was followed by a notchback version, the 400-series, in 1990. Neither was quite big enough to represent a replacement for the Montego, which therefore continued in production into 1992, but commentators widely predicted a new Rover 600/Honda Synchro model which would replace the Montego in 1992 or 1993. The Montego still had its adherents, and in the summer of 1991 it was announced that 5000 cars had been ordered for Police use in Siberia. It was surely coincidence that the abortive anti-Gorbachev coup followed a few weeks later...

Specifications

MONTEGO 1.3 1984-89
Engine four cylinder ohv transverse, 1275cc
Bore × stroke 70.6×81.3mm
Power 68bhp @ 5600rpm
Transmission four-speed manual end-on (five-speed optional), front wheel drive
Chassis unitary construction
Wheelbase 101in (2565mm)
Length 175.9in (4467mm)
Width 67.3in (1710mm)
Height 55.8in (1418mm)
Weight 2095lbs (950kg)
Suspension independent strut and coil front, trailing axle with coils rear
Brakes hydraulic, discs at front
Bodywork four-door saloon
Top speed 96mph (154km/h)
Price when introduced £5281
Total production 26,841

MONTEGO 1.6 1984 to date
As 1.3, except:
Engine four cylinder ohc transverse, 1598cc
Bore × stroke 76.2×87.6mm
Power 85bhp @ 5600rpm
Transmission four- or five-speed, automatic optional
Height estate 59.9in (1521mm)
Weight 2130-2215lbs (965-1005kg) saloon, 2250-2350lbs (1020-1065kg) estate

Bodywork four-door saloon, estate car
Top speed 102mph (165km/h)
Price when introduced £5660-£6875 (saloon), £6395-£7755 (estate)
Production to end of 1990, saloon 229,345, estate 71,858

MONTEGO 2.0 1984 to date
As 1.6, except:
Engine 1994cc
Bore × stroke 84.5×89mm
Power 102bhp @ 5500rpm (carburettor models), 117bhp @ 5500rpm (fuel injection models), 152bhp @ 5100rpm (MG Turbo)
Transmission five-speed, automatic optional (MG models manual only)
Weight 2250-2315lbs (1020-1050kg) saloon, 2350-2450lbs (1065-1110kg) estate
Top speed 108mph (174km/h) carburettor models, 115mph (185km/h) fuel injection models, 125mph (201km/h) MG Turbo
Price when introduced £7195-£8245 (saloon), £8125-£8545 (estate), £8165 (MG Saloon), £10,301 (MG Turbo saloon 1985)
Production to end of 1990, saloon 64,715, estate 24,313, Vanden Plas saloon 12,598 (1984-88), Vanden Plas estate 3,700 (1984-88), MG 37,476, MG Turbo 7,276

A slightly different grille and front spoiler were found on MG-badged versions. This is the quickest of them all, the MG Montego Turbo. Eventually the turbo engine would also be offered in the MG Maestro.

MONTEGO DIESEL 1988 to date
As 2.0, except:
Engine Turbo Diesel
Power 80bhp @ 4500rpm
Transmission five-speed only
Weight 2500lbs (1135kg) saloon, 2600lbs (1180kg) estate
Top speed 101mph (163km/h)
Price when introduced £9378-£10,499 (saloon), £10,228-£11,349 (estate)
Production to end of 1990, saloon 16,531, estate 10,121